MW01181728

（ライブラリースタンプ）

THE ACQUISITION
OF FLORIDA

NORTH KIRKWOOD MIDDLE SCHOOL
LIBRARY

MILESTONES
IN AMERICAN HISTORY

THE ACQUISITION
OF FLORIDA

AMERICA'S TWENTY-SEVENTH STATE

LIZ SONNEBORN

CHELSEA HOUSE
PUBLISHERS
An imprint of Infobase Publishing

The Acquisition of Florida

Copyright © 2009 by Infobase Publishing

All rights reserved. No part of this book may be reproduced or utilized in any form or
by any means, electronic or mechanical, including photocopying, recording, or by any
information storage or retrieval systems, without permission in writing from the publisher.
For information, contact:

Chelsea House
An imprint of Infobase Publishing
132 West 31st Street
New York, NY 10001

Library of Congress Cataloging-in-Publication Data
Sonneborn, Liz.
    The acquisition of Florida : America's Twenty-seventh State / Liz Sonneborn.
        p. cm.—(Milestones in American history)
    Includes bibliographical references and index.
    ISBN 978-1-60413-054-6 (hardcover : alk. paper)   1. Florida—History—Spanish
colony, 1784–1821—Juvenile literature.   2. Florida—History—1821–1865—Juvenile
literature.   3. United States—Foreign relations—Spain—Juvenile literature.
4. Spain—Foreign relations—United States—Juvenile literature.   5. United States—
Foreign relations—1817–1825—Juvenile literature.   6. Florida—History—To 1821—
Juvenile literature.   I. Title.   II. Series.

    F314.S696 2009
    975.9'04—dc22

                                                        2008030740

Chelsea House books are available at special discounts when purchased in bulk quantities
for businesses, associations, institutions, or sales promotions. Please call our Special Sales
Department in New York at (212) 967–8800 or (800) 322–8755.

You can find Chelsea House on the World Wide Web at http://www.chelseahouse.com

Series design by Erik Lindstrom
Cover design by Ben Peterson

Printed in the United States of America

Bang NMSG 10 9 8 7 6 5 4 3 2 1

This book is printed on acid-free paper.

All links and Web addresses were checked and verified to be correct at the time
of publication. Because of the dynamic nature of the Web, some addresses and links
may have changed since publication and may no longer be valid.

CONTENTS

Invading Spanish Florida

On March 12, 1818, a motley army crossed the boundary between the United States and East Florida, a colony then claimed by Spain. The soldiers were just beginning their mission, but they were already exhausted. On their long march to the border, they had endured bitterly cold weather and brutal rainstorms. Some wore clothing so tattered that they looked half naked. Even worse, the men were starving. They had waited for days at the American post of Fort Scott for supply ships carrying food rations, but the ships had never arrived.

The army itself was a mishmash. Some men were regular soldiers in the U.S. Army. Others were relatively untrained militiamen from Georgia and volunteers from Tennessee and Kentucky. Still others were Creek Indians who had allied themselves with the United States.

During the War of 1812, Andrew Jackson became a national war hero and was nicknamed "Old Hickory" for his toughness in battle. In 1818, while leading a ragtag regiment of hungry soldiers, Jackson was ordered to invade Florida to do battle with the Seminole Indians.

The leader of the beleaguered force was Major General Andrew Jackson. Hailing from Tennessee, Jackson was the commander of the Southern Division of the U.S. Army. To many Americans, however, he was much more than that. During the War of 1812 (official ending in 1814; unofficial ending in 1815), Jackson had become a nationally famous war hero. He was also well known as an American Indian fighter. His military campaigns against American Indians in the Southeast helped the United States to wrestle away tribal lands and open them up to white settlement. Not surprisingly, Jackson's successes had made him a popular figure among southern Americans, and that popularity had emboldened him. Ambitious and daring, he began to plot how to translate his military fame into a successful run for the White House.

Jackson had been sent on his present mission by the American secretary of war, John C. Calhoun. On the day after Christmas in 1817, Secretary Calhoun wrote a letter to Jackson in which he ordered the major general into East Florida to deal with the United States's long-festering problems with the Seminole Indians. For years, the Florida Seminole had been fighting with Americans, especially with Georgians living north of the East Florida border. When Georgians attacked the Seminole, the Seminole retaliated against Georgian settlements and settlers, which prompted more attacks by the Georgians. To end the violence on the border, Calhoun instructed Jackson to attack and subdue the Seminole. Calhoun's letter, however, said nothing about the Spanish in Florida. Perhaps he assumed that Jackson would know to steer clear of Spanish settlements. Or perhaps Calhoun neglected to mention the Spanish on purpose, with the intent of giving the impetuous Jackson a free hand to do what he wished with his invading army.

LOOKING FOR A FIGHT

One day after Jackson and his men arrived in Florida, they got a lucky break. Marching along the Apalachicola River, the soldiers met up with one of the supply ships they had been waiting for. For the first time in weeks, the soldiers enjoyed a real meal.

With their stomachs full, the men's morale improved. If anything, they proved overeager for a fight. A few soldiers captured three American Indians, whom they assumed were enemies of the United States. When one American Indian tried to escape, 50 soldiers fired their muskets at him. The gunfire got the attention of the rest of Jackson's men, who thought that they were under attack by hostile American Indians. Officers rushed to calm the situation before the men could start shooting.

The army's first chance at real combat came in late March, when it descended on the Seminole village of Tallahassee. Soldiers hoping for a great battle were disappointed, however. The Seminole had heard of Jackson's advance and had abandoned their village, escaping into the nearby countryside.

His men were starving, and many were sick with measles, but Jackson pressed on. A few days later, the army reached a village on Lake Miccosukee. Jackson organized his soldiers into right and left flanks. He hoped to surround the village by coming at it from two directions. Before the men moved forward, however, the right flank mistook the left flank for the enemy. In the confusion, the two halves of Jackson's force began firing at each other. The shots alerted the Seminole on Lake Miccosukee, and the American Indians ran away before Jackson's army could attack them. The army looted the abandoned village, making away with a huge stash of corn and herds of cattle.

TAKING OVER ST. MARKS

Jackson did not try to chase after the Seminole who fled from Lake Miccosukee. He had other ideas about what to do next. Instead of heading to another village, he led his army to St. Marks, a fort manned by Spanish soldiers charged with protecting East Florida. When Jackson reached St. Marks, he held out a white flag as a signal that he had come in peace. The Spaniards, led by their commandant, Francisco Caso y Luengo, answered by waving a white flag of their own. Caso y Luengo welcomed the Americans and allowed them to come and go from the fort as they wished.

Caso y Luengo was less than impressed by the Americans' goodwill after he received a letter from General Jackson, however. In the letter, Jackson explained that he was taking over the fort. He claimed that his action was justified under "the immutable principal of self defence."[1] As Jackson saw it, the Spanish had not subdued the Seminole or defended their border as they had promised to do in the past: "To prevent the recurrance of so gross a violation of neutrality & to exclude our savage Enemies from so strong a hold as St. Marks," he wrote, "I deem it expedient to garrison that fortress with American troops, until the close of the present war."[2]

Caso y Luengo was angered by Jackson's power play, but he hid his feelings. He responded first by congratulating Jackson on his current campaign against the Seminole. He then said that he needed to speak with his superiors in the Spanish government about the American occupation of St. Marks. While he checked with his superiors, Caso y Luengo invited the American troops to stay at St. Marks with all "good faith and harmony."[3]

In truth, the Spanish commandant was doing his best to put a good face on a humiliating situation. He knew that the Spanish government would be furious. He also knew that he did not have enough soldiers to take on Jackson's force. Ultimately, Caso y Luengo agreed to leave St. Marks with his men and head to Pensacola, the capital of Spanish-held West Florida. The Spanish surrendered the fort at St. Marks without either side firing a shot.

ON THE SUWANNEE RIVER

When Jackson took control over St. Marks, he discovered that a Scottish trader named Alexander Arbuthnot was at the fort, visiting Caso y Luengo. Arbuthnot was about 70 years old. He was well known as a friend to the Seminole, with whom he did business. To Jackson, that friendly relationship meant that Arbuthnot was an enemy. In fact, Jackson placed America's problems with the Seminole squarely on the old man's shoulders. He called Arbuthnot a "noted Scotch villain . . . who has

The Seminole lived in small villages *(above)* in Florida and were known to provide refuge to runaway slaves. After taking over St. Marks Fort, Andrew Jackson and his men slogged through the swampy Florida back-country searching for more of these villages and their inhabitants.

not only excited but fomented a continuance of the war."[4] On Jackson's orders, Arbuthnot was taken prisoner and placed in irons.

Leaving a small force at St. Marks, Jackson resumed his war on the Seminole. He headed east toward the Seminole villages on the Suwannee River. The area was also home to a large number of ex-slaves who had run away from their American owners. If his campaign succeeded, Jackson would please his southern supporters by punishing both the runaway slaves and the Seminole who gave them safe haven.

Marching to the Suwannee proved to be a long, hard slog. In the hot, wet wilderness, many of the army's horses collapsed and died. Without horses, many soldiers had to move on foot through thick vegetation over mucky ground. Food rations ran low, and the men were overwhelmed by hunger and exhaustion.

Because of his army's slow progress, Jackson could not expect to keep its advance a secret. Predictably, when the army finally arrived at the Suwannee, the riverside villages were empty of Seminole. There were ample foodstuffs to steal, however, including a healthy haul from a store operated by Alexander Arbuthnot's son John.

CAPTURING AMBRISTER

While it was camped along the Suwannee, Jackson's army received a group of unexpected visitors. One night, four men, including one in a British uniform, walked confidently toward the Americans' campfires. The men assumed they were entering a Seminole camp. When they realized their mistake, they tried to escape, but the Americans chased them down and captured them.

To the Americans, one of the men was great prize. He was Robert Christie Ambrister, a 31-year-old ex–Royal Marine from the British Navy. He had been working for some unsavory British adventurers in Florida who were plotting to harass the Spanish authorities. Ambrister's job was to train ex-slaves and Indians in military maneuvers.

On one member of Ambrister's party, the Americans found a letter from Alexander Arbuthnot to his son John. In it, the old trader warned that Jackson was on his way to the Suwannee. Arbuthnot told his son to take all the merchandise he could from his store and get out before the American army arrived. In the letter, the elder Arbuthnot also included a message for Chief Bowlegs, a leader of the Suwannee Seminole: "Tell my friend Bowleck [sic] that it is throwing away his people to attempt to resist such a powerful force."[5]

ON TRIAL

During their time in Florida, Jackson's men had encountered few Seminole. Despite this, after the Suwannee campaign, Jackson declared that his war with the American Indians was over.

All of his men were tired, and many were sick. It was also late April, the beginning of what Jackson called the "sickly season."[6] In Florida, it soon would be so hot and humid that a wide-scale military campaign would be hard to wage.

Jackson sent the Georgia militia and his Creek Indian allies home. Jackson's army now consisted of Regular Army soldiers and Tennessee volunteers. Both groups were extremely loyal to Jackson. Jackson wrote to Calhoun to say that after he returned to St. Marks, he and the rest of his men would soon come back to the United States.

When he reached St. Marks, Jackson immediately turned his attention to a piece of unfinished business. He appointed a special court of officers that included five Tennessee volunteers who were especially close to Jackson. These men were given the task of trying Alexander Arbuthnot and Robert Ambrister, who were charged with crimes against the United States. Jackson held that these crimes were capital offenses deserving of the death penalty. The court had no real legal standing, but Jackson did not care. He maintained that "the laws of war did not apply to conflicts with savages."[7] This assertion conveniently gave him license to do whatever he wanted.

At the trial, Arbuthnot pleaded not guilty. He explained that he had done nothing wrong in befriending the Seminole, who were his business partners and customers. He had tried to protect them from exploitation by Americans and by his British kinsmen, he added, to keep the peace among all parties. How, he asked, could that possibly make him an enemy of the United States? Ambrister had a weaker case, and he knew it. Instead of defending his actions, he threw himself on the mercy of the makeshift court.

After two days, on April 28, 1818, the court announced its verdict: Both men were guilty. The next morning, Arbuthnot was to be hanged and Ambrister was to face a firing squad.

After the sentences were delivered, however, one member of the court voiced his uneasiness with Ambrister's fate. This prompted the court to reopen the matter. Ambrister was a young military man, much like the Americans who were holding him in judgment. Sympathizing with the ex–Royal Marine, the members of the court decided that Ambrister simply had been in the wrong place at the wrong time. They reduced his sentence to 50 lashes and a year of hard labor.

SEIZING CONTROL

Jackson was exasperated. He had set up his court to do his bidding, not to come up with its own ruling. Annoyed, Jackson ignored the court's sentence. Under his orders, both Arbuthnot and Ambrister were executed the next day.

Jackson also went back on his promise to Calhoun. Instead of returning to the United States with his army, he ordered his men to continue their campaign in Florida. This, however, was not the campaign against the Seminoles that Calhoun had sanctioned, but the one against the Spanish that Jackson had initiated on his own. Jackson was determined to claim the largest city in Spanish Florida for America. He led his men west to Pensacola.

Jackson's 1818 invasion of Spanish Florida is just one episode, although an important one, in the larger story of how Florida became part of the United States. This incident illustrates well how the long and chaotic struggle for control of this valuable territory involved a wide variety of people of several different nationalities who acted with many different motives.

Before the founding of the United States, the Spanish, the French, and the British all coveted Florida. Additionally, the many native peoples who lived in the area fought to remove these outsiders from the region that their ancestors had called home for centuries. After the United States was formed, the situation grew even more complicated. American settlers and politicians, as well as pirates and adventurers, were added to the mix. All were trying to seize a piece of Florida for personal fortune and professional gain. Only after a drawn-out contest in which the competitors relied as much on diplomatic finesse as on military might did America finally win full control of the prize called Florida. The acquisition of Florida proved to be a pivotal moment, not only in the history of Florida, but also in the history of the United States.

The Flowery Land

In early March 1513, explorer Juan Ponce de León set out with three ships on a voyage in search of a wondrous land. The 39-year-old Spaniard had been the governor of Puerto Rico, a Caribbean island colony claimed by the Spanish government. There, Ponce de León had heard curious stories about a lush island to the northwest. He wanted to see for himself whether there was any truth behind the tales.

On April 2, Ponce de León and his men found what they were looking for. The ships anchored off the coast of what they assumed was an island but was, in fact, part of a large peninsula. Once ashore, Ponce de León was impressed by the new land's beautiful vegetation. He dubbed his discovery *La Florida*, Spanish for "the flowery land." After exploring the coast, Ponce de León sailed to Spain. There, he was given permission to colonize Florida.

Despite discoverying gold and colonizing Puerto Rico, Juan Ponce de León is most famous for leading an expedition into Florida. Legend has it that he was looking for a mythical fountain of youth. Although most historians discount this story, during his travels in Florida Ponce de León possibly did come upon a natural spring located in what is now St. Augustine.

SPANIARDS COME TO *LA FLORIDA*

Of course, when Ponce de León and his men first arrived in Florida, they did not enter an uninhabited landscape. Florida had been home to many different American Indian peoples for thousands of years. Tribes native to Florida included the Timucua, the Apalachee, and the Calusa. With its warm climate and plentiful food supplies, Florida provided a comfortable environment that allowed these tribes to thrive.

Not surprisingly, the American Indians' desire to protect their homelands ran strong—a fact that Ponce de León learned on his second voyage to Florida. In 1521, the explorer returned with two ships and 200 men. The presence of this impressive army was not enough to dissuade the area's American Indians from attacking the foreigners, however. During the fight, Ponce de León was struck by an arrow. Later, back in Spanish Cuba, he died from his wound.

Despite Ponce de León's fate, Florida was enough of a prize to attract a series of Spanish expeditions. The most formidable of these was led by Hernando de Soto in the spring of 1539. De Soto arrived in what is now Tampa Bay with nearly 600 soldiers. He was on a search for gold, inspired by other Spanish adventurers such as Hernán Cortés and Francisco Pizarro, who earlier had found great stores of this precious metal elsewhere in the Americas. Like these men, de Soto had a cruel streak. He battled viciously with the tribes of the region before deciding that there was no gold to be had in Florida.

De Soto continued his march through what is now the American Southeast, fighting American Indians all the way in his search for wealth. During de Soto's conquest, his men spread European diseases, such as measles and smallpox, among the American Indians that they met. The American Indians did not have natural immunities to these unfamiliar germs. As a result, American Indian populations, even after the briefest contact with de Soto's men, suffered horrible epidemics that lasted for decades. With all the havoc he caused, de Soto never did find gold. He did, however, reach the Mississippi River. He and his men may, in fact, have been the first Europeans to see that great river. In 1542, when he became ill and died, de Soto's men are said to have buried him in the river's deep waters.

During the sixteenth century, bad luck seemed to fall on all the Spaniards who ventured to Florida. Pánfilo de Narváez was appointed governor by the Spanish king but drowned during a storm at sea in 1528. Luis Cancer de Barbastro, a Spanish Dominican friar, tried to convert the American Indians of Florida to Christianity but instead was killed by them in 1549. Explorer Tristan de Luna abandoned his attempts to establish a Spanish colony in Florida when his men mutinied in 1560.

THE FRENCH AT FORT CAROLINE

Undeterred by a half century of Spanish failures, a French expedition arrived in Florida in 1564. Its members were Huguenots—Protestants who faced persecution in their Catholic homeland. Knowing that the French king, Charles IX, wanted to gain a foothold in North America, the Huguenot leaders made a proposal to the crown. They asked for help in establishing a permanent French settlement in Florida that would provide a safe haven for all of the Huguenots. With Charles's approval, several hundred settlers sailed to the mouth of the St. Johns River, where they built a small village and a fort. They called it Fort Caroline.

The French settlement struggled to survive. The Timucua Indians posed a constant threat, and as the settlers' provisions ran low, they were in danger of starving to death. They were ready to abandon the colony when, in August 1565, French ships with supplies and hundreds of fresh recruits arrived along the Florida coast.

The ships also attracted the attention of the Spanish. Spain already was anxious about France's challenge to their claim to Florida. Now, the Spanish were worried that the arrival of supplies and more French colonists might save the floundering Fort

St. Augustine was a Spanish settlement established by the military leader Pedro Menéndez de Avilés. After destroying the French population in Florida, Menéndez concentrated on expanding St. Augustine, which soon became an important Spanish town in North America.

Caroline settlement. On the order of King Philip II of Spain, Pedro Menéndez de Avilés, the Spanish governor of Florida, established a military base on the coast and prepared to attack the French ships.

ESTABLISHING ST. AUGUSTINE AND PENSACOLA

Before Menéndez could attack, however, fate intervened. A storm blew up and scattered the French fleet. Menéndez took advantage of the situation and marched an army toward Fort Caroline. Menéndez's soldiers launched a vicious attack on the French settlement, killing all but about 50 of the inhabitants. Menéndez's men then turned their attention to the new French recruits who had survived the storm. Again, Menéndez's men murdered as many of the French as they could. The slaughter sent a strong message to France about the hazard of trying to intrude on Spanish claims in North America.

After the destruction of Fort Caroline, Menéndez focused on building up his coastal base, a settlement that became known as St. Augustine. Unlike France's ill-fated experiment, the community of St. Augustine was going to last. In fact, it became the first permanent European settlement in North America. By the time England established its first permanent settlement at Jamestown, Virginia, in 1607, St. Augustine was a 42-year-old town with a fort, a church, and dozens of houses and shops.

In 1698, the Spanish established another important town in Florida. Called Pensacola, it was located on the Gulf of Mexico near the Perdido River, which today marks the western border of the Florida Panhandle. At Pensacola, the Spanish built a fort to protect Spanish Florida from the French, who were staking claim to the Mississippi Valley. Because they were separated by about 400 miles, there was little contact between the Spaniards at St. Augustine and those at Pensacola.

A STRUGGLING COLONY

Throughout the late sixteenth and seventeenth centuries, the Spanish struggled to make Florida a profitable colony. Unlike some other Spanish-held lands in the Americas, Florida did not have stores of gold, gems, or minerals. But it did have a pleasant climate and some land that was good for farming and ranching. The Spanish had only limited success growing cash crops such as tobacco and cotton. They also tried but failed to develop various other industries, from producing dye to harvesting silk to exporting smoked fish. As a result, the Spanish in Florida were dependent on food and supplies that were sent to them each year by Spanish officials in Mexico City.

During this period, Florida was ruled by a governor. Answering to him was a number of lesser officials. Their appointments all were authorized by the king of Spain. Many officials received their jobs because of their connections to the court. Some posts were held for life and then passed down to a family member. For the most part, the officials in Spanish Florida were corrupt.

They were more interested in skimming off whatever money they could than in working to build the colony.

Unlike American Indians in some other Spanish colonies, the American Indians in Florida were relatively undisturbed by the Spanish. Officials in St. Augustine required tribes there to supply them with goods and labor. Elsewhere, however, Florida's Indians largely were left alone. With relatively few Spaniards in Florida, the Spanish did not want to antagonize the native population. As a show of friendship, the Spanish governors often addressed tribe leaders as "my sons and cousins."[1]

The Spaniards who had the most interaction with Florida's American Indians were missionaries. These were Catholic priests who came to Florida to convert the American Indians to Christianity. The priests constructed complexes of buildings called missions, where converts gathered and worked. At the missions, American Indians were instructed in European farming methods and were trained in crafts such as weaving and carpentry. The priests also taught them non-American Indian customs and, often, the Spanish language. By the mid-seventeenth century, there were more than 30 missions in Florida. The mission system had an American Indian population of about 25,000.

In the early eighteenth century, foreign invaders all but destroyed the Florida missions. The invaders were led by James Moore, the governor of South Carolina, an English colony to the north of Florida. In 1702, and again in 1704, English raiders attacked the missions, killing many of the American Indian and Spaniards there. The English even burned several priests at the stake. The raiders took several thousand Indians captive and sold them into slavery.

THE FRENCH AND INDIAN WAR

When Ponce de León claimed Florida for Spain, its boundaries were vague, although it was thought to stretch from present-day Canada in the north to present-day Texas in the west. By the eighteenth century, however, as more English and French settlers arrived in North America, the area that Spain claimed as Florida had been greatly reduced. The English had established colonies along the Atlantic coast and were moving westward. The French had claimed the Mississippi Valley and were expanding eastward. When these European forces collided and began competing for the same land, fighting broke out. The conflict eventually escalated into what became known as the French and Indian War (1754–1763). The war's name came from the fact that many Indian groups joined with the French to battle the British. As the war progressed, Spain felt obligated to take a side. Fearing Great Britain the most, in 1761, Spain allied itself with France.

The decision proved to be a mistake for Spain. France lost the war. According to the Treaty of Paris of 1763, which ended the conflict, France had to sign over its North American territory east of the Mississippi to Great Britain. In 1762, in gratitude for Spain's allegiance, France had given Spain control over the port of New Orleans and over its lands west of the Mississippi, all of which were then called Louisiana.

During the treaty negotiations, Spain found itself in a difficult position. In the course of the war, the British had taken control of Havana, the port city of the Spanish colony on Cuba. Great Britain agreed to return this valuable port to Spain on one condition: that Spain gave Florida to Great Britain in return. The Treaty of Paris set the western boundary of Florida at the Mississippi River. The new British colony of Florida included all of the present-day state of Florida and parts of what today are the states of Alabama, Mississippi, and Louisiana.

THE BRITISH ERA

The British immediately decided that Florida was too large for one local government to administer. They split it into two colonies—West Florida and East Florida. West Florida was the narrow

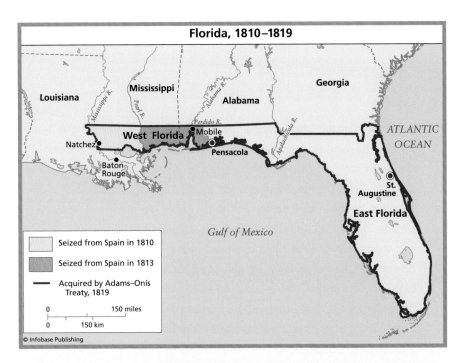

Florida, 1810–1819

After the French and Indian War, Spain relinquished Florida to the British in exchange for control of Havana, Cuba. The British immediately took charge and divided the area into two parts: West and East Florida. The territory of West Florida included pieces of land in the modern-day states of Alabama, Mississippi, and Louisiana.

strip of land between the Mississippi and the Apalachicola rivers. It included the towns of Mobile, Baton Rouge, and Natchez, but its capital was Pensacola. East Florida was all of the Florida territory east of the Apalachicola. Its capital was St. Augustine.

When the transfer of power took place, many Spaniards left Florida and headed to Cuba. The population of the British Floridas became a hodgepodge of newly arrived British immigrants, their African slaves, and remnants of various American Indian groups. Increasingly, members of the Creek Indian confederacy from present-day Georgia and Alabama also headed south to settle in the Floridas. There, they became known as the Seminole.

WILLIAM BARTRAM'S TRAVELS IN THE BRITISH FLORIDAS

In the years before the American Revolution, British writer William Bartram traveled through what today is the southeastern part of the United States. In 1765, just two years after Great Britain acquired East and West Florida, Bartram made his first expedition into this territory. He came as a companion to his father, John Bartram, who was the first professional botanist in the American colonies.

William Bartram decided to remain in the Floridas. For a time, he operated an indigo farm. He also used his skills as a draftsman to draw maps of the Florida coast. In 1773, Bartram obtained funds to conduct a botanical study in the Floridas. For several years, he explored the area as well as several nearby colonies. In 1791, after returning to his home in Pennsylvania, Bartram published an account of his adventures in a book titled *Travels Through North & South Carolina, Georgia, East & West Florida.* In this excerpt, Bartram concentrates his considerable powers of observation on the Florida alligator. He tries to describe it to British readers who know little or nothing about this exotic animal.

> The alligator when full grown is a very large and terrible creature, and of prodigious strength, activity and swiftness in the water. I have seen them twenty feet in length, and some are supposed to be twenty-two or twenty-three feet; their body is as large as that of a horse; their shape exactly resembles that of a lizard. . . . [T]he whole body is covered with horny plates or squammae, impenetrable . . . even to a rifle ball. . . . Only the upper jaw moves, which they raise almost perpendicular, so as to form a right angle with the lower one. . . . [W]hen they clap

Like the Spanish, the British tried to make the Floridas profitable but had only limited success. The economy of West Florida was based on the fur trade; that of East Florida revolved

their jaws together it causes a surprising noise, like that which is made by forcing a heavy plank with violence upon the ground, and may be heard at a great distance.

But what is yet more surprising to a stranger, is the incredible loud and terrifying roar, which they are capable of making, especially in the spring season, their breeding time; it most resembles very heavy distant thunder, not only shaking the air and waters, but causing the earth to tremble; and when hundreds and thousands are roaring at the same time, you can scarcely be persuaded, but that the whole globe is violently and dangerously agitated.

An old champion, who is perhaps absolute sovereign of a little lake or lagoon, . . . darts forth from the reedy coverts all at once, on the surface of the waters, in a right line; at first seemingly as rapid as lightning . . . ; he now swells himself by drawing in wind and water through his mouth . . . [I]t is immediately forced out again through his mouth and nostrils, with a loud noise, brandishing his tail in the air, and the vapour ascending from his nostrils like smoke. At other times, when swolen to an extent ready to burst, his head and tail lifted up, he spins or twirls round on the surface of the water. He acts his part like an Indian chief when rehearsing his feats of war. . . . [T]he exhibition is continued by others who dare to step forth, and strive to excel each other, to gain the attention of the favourite female.*

*William Bartram, Travels Through North & South Carolina, Georgia, East & West Florida. *Philadelphia: James & Johnson, 1791, pp. 128–129.*

around farming. In East Florida, the British built large plantations on which they grew rice and the plant from which indigo, a valuable blue dye, was produced. The first British lieutenant governor of East Florida, John Moultrie, established Bella Vista, a plantation with a 10-room stone mansion surrounded by gardens and fish ponds. The plantation produced indigo, rice, and other crops.

Under the British, St. Augustine became well-known for its wild atmosphere. One visitor noted that "luxury and debauchery reigned amidst scarcity."[2] Governor James Grant gleefully wrote to a friend that "there is not so gay a Town in America as this is at present, the People [are] Musick and Dancing mad."[3] Apparently, some of the inhabitants of St. Augustine also were mad for alcohol. During Grant's first year in office, he and visitors to his home imbibed more than 230 gallons of rum and 1,200 bottles of wine.

THE AMERICAN REVOLUTION

Immigration to the Floridas grew steadily as the British government gave more and more land grants in East and West Florida to retired British soldiers. After the American Revolution (1775–1783) broke out, however, the number of British immigrants to the Floridas soared. In 1776, thirteen British colonies in North America declared their independence from their mother country and established the United States of America. The two Floridas chose to side with Great Britain. As a result, many Tories (colonists who remained loyal to Great Britain) fled from the rebellious colonies to the Floridas. In East Florida alone, the British population rose from 6,000 to 17,000 during the war years.

The British army stationed soldiers along the Florida border to protect the loyal colonies. The area did not see much fighting until 1779, when Spain allied itself with the American rebels. In that year, Bernardo de Gálvez, the governor of Spanish Louisiana, led a force into West Florida to fight the British troops guarding the towns of Baton Rouge, Mobile, and Pensacola. In May 1781, after he took Pensacola, Gálvez declared that he had reclaimed all of West Florida for Spain.

The end of the American Revolution came two years later with the signing of the Treaty of Paris of 1783. The American victors rewarded their Spanish allies, not only by recognizing their control over West Florida, but also by restoring their jurisdiction over East Florida. After 20 years of British rule, the Floridas once again were in the hands of the Spanish.

Seizing West Florida

As soon as the Spanish took over the two Floridas, they saw that holding onto these territories would be a long-term challenge. To the north, land-hungry American settlers already were eyeing the Floridas. The Spanish needed a strategy to keep them from creeping over the border and claiming Florida territory on behalf of the United States.

Promoting trade was one part of Spain's plan to solidify its claim to the Floridas. Instead of expelling English traders from the region, the Spanish authorities encouraged them to stay. The authorities were particularly supportive of the firm Panton, Leslie and Company, which had controlled most of the local American Indian trade. Spain hoped that if trade flourished in Florida, the territories' mixed population of Spaniards, Britons, and American Indians would live together peacefully and support Spanish rule.

Spain's strategy in Florida also focused on immigration. After the American Revolution, Americans started moving into West Florida, attracted by the warm climate and fertile land. Because the authorities in Florida did not have the manpower to stop them, the Spanish government adopted a different tactic. Instead of trying to stop American immigration, the government encouraged it. Beginning in 1790, the king of Spain offered land grants to Americans who were willing to move to Florida permanently. In exchange for the land, the Americans had to swear allegiance to the king and baptize their children in the Catholic Church.

PINCKNEY'S TREATY

The Spanish hoped that this plan would fill the Floridas with grateful citizens who would remain loyal to the Spanish government. Many people doubted that the Americans who were heading into Florida would be so submissive, however. Among the doubters was Thomas Jefferson, who served as President George Washington's secretary of state. Jefferson wrote to the president about the Florida immigration policy. He explained to Washington that he believed the plan would backfire on the Spanish and perhaps help the United States take over the Floridas: "I wish 10,000 of our inhabitants would accept the invitation. It would be the means of delivering to us peaceably what must otherwise cost us a war. In the meantime, we may complain of the seduction of our inhabitants just enough to make the Spanish believe it is a very wise policy for them."[1]

From its earliest days, the U.S. government wanted the Floridas. American officials were attracted not only by the territories' rich farmlands, but also by their geography. The Floridas provided access to the Gulf of Mexico. The United States envied this access because it gave Spain substantial control over sea-trade routes in the region. American officials also were uncomfortable with a foreign power having control over these territories. If Spain ever wanted to attack the southern United

NORTH KIRKWOOD MIDDLE SCHOOL
LIBRARY

States, Florida was a perfect place in which to establish military bases.

From 1783 on, the United States was up front about its interest in the Floridas. For 12 years, it argued with Spain about the region's northern border. The dispute finally was settled in 1795 by the Treaty of Friendship, Limits, and Navigation Between Spain and the United States. This agreement also was known as the Treaty of San Lorenzo and as Pinckney's Treaty, after the U.S. diplomat, Thomas Pinckney, who oversaw the negotiations. Bowing to American pressure, Spain agreed to set the border between the United States and Spanish Florida at the 31st parallel. Spain also promised to allow Americans to store goods at the port city of New Orleans in the Spanish territory of Louisiana and to freely navigate the Mississippi River. Both Spain and the United States agreed to keep the peace with American Indians living along the border.

THE LOUISIANA PURCHASE

The treaty was a victory for the United States, but it did little to subdue the Americans' desire for control over the Floridas. This desire became even more urgent in 1800, when Spain, pressured by the French ruler Napoleon Bonaparte, transferred power over Louisiana to France by the Treaty of San Ildefonso. Two years later, the Spanish agent in New Orleans cut off American access to storage warehouses in the city. This violation of Pinckney's Treaty outraged many Americans.

Thomas Jefferson was now the president, and he decided to act. He sent his friend James Monroe on a diplomatic mission to France. Jefferson authorized Monroe to offer France $10 million for both New Orleans and West Florida. Before Monroe arrived, however, Napoleon made an offer of his own. In discussions with American diplomat Robert Livingston, Napoleon proposed selling all of Louisiana to the United States for $15 million.

Claiming that the Louisiana Purchase *(seen above)* violated the terms of the Treaty of San Ildefonso, the Spanish government vehemently opposed France's sale of this vast tract of land to the United States. When the borders of the Louisiana Purchase were determined, this land purchase would double the size of the United States.

In 1803, Jefferson agreed to purchase Louisiana. The purchase doubled the size of the United States. At the time, it was not clear exactly where the borders of this vast new territory lay. During the negotiations, however, France had made one point crystal clear: Spanish-held West Florida was not part of the Louisiana Purchase.

When the Spanish learned about the Louisiana Purchase, they were livid, and understandably so. Spain claimed that France had violated the 1800 treaty that had transferred

Louisiana from Spain to France. First, the Spanish asserted, the agreement clearly stated that France could not transfer Louisiana to a third party without getting Spain's permission, and France had not done this. Second, in the treaty, Napoleon had promised to give the Duke of Parma (the brother-in-law of Spain's King Carlos IV) the throne of the kingdom of Tuscany. Because Napoleon had neglected to make the duke the king of Tuscany, the Spanish argued, the transfer agreement was null and void. By Spanish logic, Louisiana did not belong to France, and France could not sell what it did not own.

President Jefferson did not bother to argue the point. However shady the Louisiana deal was, he was happy to make it. Jefferson simply ignored Spain's protests, confident that the Spanish would not go to war over Louisiana.

EYEING WEST FLORIDA

With Spain's military weakness in mind, some Americans began to claim that Louisiana included the part of West Florida between the Mississippi and Perdido rivers. One of those who made this dubious claim was U.S. negotiator Robert Livingston, who based his interpretation on maps that dated from the early eighteenth century. Spain, however, countered quite rightly that, according to newer maps that dated from 1763, when Great Britain transferred the Floridas to Spain, the contested stretch of West Florida was most definitely part of that territory and not part of Louisiana.

Despite the evidence to the contrary, the seeds of this idea—that the land between the rivers was part of Louisiana—were sown. America's leaders continued to claim that, with the Louisiana Purchase, the United States had bought much of West Florida. This claim helped to convince Americans that, one way or another, the United States would have control over West Florida in the near future.

President Jefferson decided that the time was right to make a bold power play. With his encouragement, in 1804, the House of Representatives passed the Mobile Act. The act allowed the federal government to establish a customs district in the area of Mobile Bay in West Florida. In essence, the act stated that the United States had legal jurisdiction over areas in West Florida, even though this region was still regarded as Spanish territory.

With the Mobile Act, Jefferson was trying to bully Spain into surrendering this disputed stretch of land. But the Marquis de Casa Yrujo, a Spanish diplomat in the United States, refused to give in. He spoke out against Jefferson's actions, thereby foiling the president's hope of making a quick and easy land grab. Rather than risk war with Spain, Jefferson backed down. In his annual address to Congress later that year, Jefferson suggested that the whole issue had been nothing but a minor misunderstanding with Spain.

NEGOTIATING WITH SPAIN

Jefferson did not forget about the Floridas, however. He sent James Monroe to Spain to try to make a deal for them in early 1805, but talks quickly stalled. Because Spain sensed that Jefferson would not try to take the Floridas by force, the Spanish officials felt no pressure to negotiate with Monroe.

Any hope of making a deal with Spain was further dashed in 1808. After several years of battling neighboring countries, Napoleon Bonaparte of France invaded Spain and placed his brother Joseph on the Spanish throne. The United States refused to recognize this new government and broke off diplomatic relations with Spain.

In the same year, James Madison was elected president. Like Jefferson, Madison wanted to find a way to annex the Floridas. Because of the political landscape in Spain, however, diplomacy was no longer a viable strategy. Madison could send an army into Florida, but if he did he would risk both a drawn-out conflict and international condemnation for invading a foreign land. Luckily for Madison, a third option soon presented itself:

Like his predecessor, Thomas Jefferson, President James Madison *(above)* was determined to acquire both West and East Florida from Spain. When negotiations broke down between the two governments, Madison took advantage of a popular rebellion to send U.S. troops to occupy West Florida.

In 1810, Americans in West Florida staged their own revolt against the Spanish authorities.

It was not the first time that Americans had tried to take over West Florida. In the summer of 1804, three brothers—Nathan, Reuben, and Samuel Kemper—had staged a series of raids in the region. The Kempers had declared that they were trying to destroy Spanish rule and invited other Floridians to join their campaign. The brothers tried to present themselves as revolutionaries, but their neighbors saw them as the leaders of a gang of drunken outlaws who were menacing their communities. Instead of allying themselves with the Kempers, most Floridians—Spanish and American alike—cooperated with Spanish authorities to capture the brothers and end their crime spree.

THE REPUBLIC OF WEST FLORIDA

By 1810, more Americans had settled in West Florida. These settlers felt less and less allegiance to the local Spanish authorities, which had proved ineffective in dealing with the odd assortment of raiders and bandits who also gravitated to the region. By this time, to the annoyance of some prominent Floridians, the Spanish also were placing tighter regulations on land grants. In addition, Americans in West Florida were nervous about the political shifts in Spain. They were wary of the French and did not know what to expect from a Spanish government under Napoleon's control.

In the summer of 1810, hundreds of West Florida planters living near the town of Baton Rouge came together to demand self-government. In meetings both secret and public, they decided to declare their independence from Spanish rule. When it became clear that Spain would resist their efforts, the rebels turned to the United States for help. Represented by John Rhea, they asked President Madison for a loan to finance their republic, which they hoped would eventually be annexed by the United States.

Madison refused the rebels' requests, but the revolt continued. On September 23, 1810, an armed group of rebels took over the fort at Baton Rouge, which the Spanish surrendered without a fight. Three days later, the rebel leaders signed a declaration of independence. Fulwar Skipwith, a wealthy planter and former diplomat, was elected president of what the rebels called the Republic of West Florida. Over the Baton Rouge fort, the rebels raised the republic's flag, which bore a single white star in a field of blue. Many years later, during the American Civil War (1861–1865), the same flag—nicknamed the Bonnie Blue—was adopted by the Confederate States of America.

SENDING IN THE TROOPS

President Madison was a little annoyed by what was happening in West Florida. He still hoped, one way or another, to take both Floridas from Spain all at once. The president feared that the rebellion would get in the way of his plan.

It was clear to Madison, however, that he had to do something. By the terms of Article 1, Section 8, of the U.S. Constitution, Congress has the exclusive power to declare war. Congress was out of session, and Madison did not want to wait. Without congressional approval, Madison ordered federal troops to occupy the area of West Florida between the Mississippi and Perdido rivers.

To many, Madison's action looked like an illegal military invasion of Spanish territory. Madison tried to sell the occupation as an act of self-defense. He trotted out the questionable assertion that by the terms of the Louisiana Purchase, the region actually was U.S. territory. He claimed he had every right as president to send in troops to quell the unrest there. No matter how flimsy his justification, Madison guessed correctly that the government of Spain was in such turmoil that it could not organize a response to his land grab. On Decem-

(continues on page 35)

"VERUS" OBJECTS TO THE AMERICAN OCCUPATION OF WEST FLORIDA

In 1810, after a popular revolution against Spanish rule in West Florida, President James Madison sent U.S. troops into the area. The brazen challenge to Spanish claims to West Florida outraged Luis de Onís (1769–1830), a Spanish diplomat who had been in the United States since 1809. Because of upheavals in the Spanish government, Washington officials initially refused to deal with Onís. That did not stop him from criticizing the United States's behavior toward Spain, however. He did so in a series of pamphlets that he wrote under the pseudonym "Verus"—a name taken from the Latin word for "true." In this excerpt from a "Verus" pamphlet published in 1812, Onís poses as an American as he attacks President Madison's decision to keep U.S. soldiers in West Florida.

> [A]ll the winding and pompous sophisms, brought out . . . to [justify the occupation of Florida,] an act so much subversive of the law of nations, and as utterly contrary to the most sacred principles of public morals and good faith, as to those of our neutrality and honour, were, I believe crushed thereby in such a manner, that no man of common sense could fail to laugh at them. . . . However, the occupation of West Florida has been carried into execution; and new measures and exertions do appear from day to day, calculating to bring the violence and hostilities against the Spanish nation to the highest degree: so that every citizen of America, who has the honour and welfare of his country at heart, cannot be insensible to such baneful abuses, and to such a fatal mischievousness. Very often the human mind, when waxed warm with ambition and pride, acknowledges neither rules nor duties. . . .

(continues)

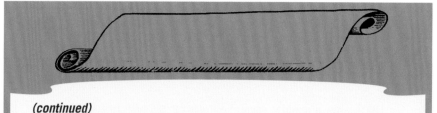

(continued)

Our administration think the possession of Florida suits the [American leaders'] ambitious purposes; consequently, while they give to the Spanish government the most positive assurances, that they will never permit any American citizen to commit an act of hostility against the territory of Florida, and promise up on their honour, and that of the United States, to chastise severely every aggressor; they break out in the most violent measures, and give orders not only for the invasion of that province, but . . . to join the insurgents, and to bring the torches of revolution, plunder, carnage, and desolution, though the defenceless regions of our honest and peaceful neighbours. . . .

Citizens of America, either democrats or federalists, we are all brethren, and all equally concerned in the safety and happiness of our republic. It is settled on the venerable principles of justice, good faith, moderation, and honour; but alas! you must confess, that they are undermined, and that the majestic structure of the virtues, and the wisdom of our fathers, is much endangered as to be already tottering, and ready to fall. The measures and exertions adopted by our [president] against the Spanish nation, are to be heard with astonishment and execration in every quarter of the world.*

Luis de Onís, Observations on the Conduct of our Executive Towards Spain (1812), pp. 20–21.

(continued from page 32)

ber 10, 1810, at Baton Rouge, the blue flag of the Republic of West Florida was replaced by the American stars and stripes. During the years that followed, the area once known as West

Florida was incorporated into four present-day states—Louisiana, Mississippi, Alabama, and Florida.

The story of the United States's annexation of the Republic of West Florida offered several provocative and powerful lessons to Madison and later presidents. It proved that Spain's hold over its lands in North America was tenuous at best. Perhaps more importantly, however, it made clear that a president who was willing to take bold action could seize a piece of the Spanish empire without paying a political price.

Three Wars

In the wake of the 1810 rebellion in West Florida, the federal government announced a bold new policy. On January 15, 1811, Congress passed the secret No Transfer Resolution. This declaration authorized the president to take control of Spanish territories, including the Floridas, "in the event of any attempt to occupy the said territories . . . by any foreign government."[1]

The phrasing was peculiar. After all, even though West Florida was now occupied by American troops, the Floridas already were officially controlled by a "foreign government"—the government of Spain. As the recent conflict in West Florida showed, however, the Spanish were losing control of their lands in the Americas. U.S. officials feared that the British might try to take advantage of Spanish weakness. The No Transfer Resolution, therefore, was meant to prepare for and prevent a British land grab, particularly in East Florida.

LOOKING ACROSS THE BORDER

Trouble also was brewing along the Florida border. Increasingly, American settlers in Georgia to the north were hungry to take over the rich lands to the south. Convinced that the area should be under American control, the Georgia settlers had little respect for the Spanish authorities in Florida.

The Georgians also were angry that the Spaniards did nothing when African slaves ran away from their American masters and headed for refuge in Spanish-held territory. The escaped slaves sometimes joined communities of Seminole Indians. The Seminole were a combination of American Indian peoples. Some were from small Florida tribes, but most were former members of the Creek Indian Confederacy, the dominant American Indian group in present-day Georgia and Alabama. Beginning in about the middle of the eighteenth century, the Creek began heading south to Florida. Many fled their own homelands to get away from the white settlers there.

American southerners, especially Georgians close to the Florida border, were frightened that bands of Seminole might raid their farms and homes. They also lived in constant fear of slave revolts. Many settlers worried that runaway slaves in Spanish Florida would obtain firearms there and use them to stage attacks on southern plantations.

Americans also were concerned that northeastern Florida had become a magnet for outlaws. The Embargo Act of 1807 forbade the importation of foreign goods into the United States. Smugglers, hoping to get around this law, took over Amelia Island, which was located just off the East Florida coast, near the border with Georgia. Fear of outlaw merchants and pirates only increased the desire of southern Americans to see the Floridas placed firmly under the control of the United States. By 1812, newspapers in the southern states routinely called for East Florida's annexation.

THE PATRIOT WAR

Among the southerners most disturbed by the situation was George Mathews. A former governor of Georgia, the 72-year-old Mathews decided to take matters into his own hands by invading East Florida and stirring up a revolt against Spanish rule. He gathered an army of about 80 men—mostly Georgians and a few Floridians—who called themselves Patriots. Determined to liberate East Florida, the Patriot army crossed the Georgia-Florida border on March 10, 1812.

Mathews hoped to stir up the local residents, but few were interested in his revolution. The majority of Americans in East Florida were happy with the Spanish authorities, who, for the most part, left them alone to live as they chose. The East Florida Americans did not foresee much advantage in living under the laws and regulations that the United States likely would impose on them. Even after Mathews tried to bribe residents to join his army, the Floridians still showed only muted enthusiasm for his cause.

Without the Floridian Americans' support, Mathews and his men soldiered on. They headed toward the port town of Fernandina, on Amelia Island, and landed there on March 17. Mathews declared Fernandina a free and independent republic.

That independence did not last long. On March 18, Mathews ceded Amelia to the United States. American troops from a military base at Point Petre, Georgia, took over the island. The troops had been sent by President Madison, who saw an opportunity in the Patriot War. Madison thought that if he provided Mathews's men with a little military support, they might be able to establish control over all of East Florida, just as rebels had taken control of West Florida in 1810.

MADISON BACKS AWAY

At first, it seemed as if the president would get his wish. Expanding the conflict, the Patriots, closely followed by the U.S. Army,

As a young man, future U.S. president Andrew Jackson fought the British in the American Revolution. In the War of 1812, Jackson again battled British troops. During this conflict, he led a regiment from Tennessee, depicted in the painting above.

set out to take St. Augustine, the capital of Spanish East Florida. On June 25, the House of Representatives lent its support to the Patriot War by authorizing Madison to annex the region.

A week earlier, at Madison's request, Congress had issued a formal declaration of war against the British. This conflict, known as the War of 1812 (1812–1814), had a number of causes. The United States wanted to put an end to British interference in the American sea trade, especially the practice of forcing American sailors into service in the British Navy. Many Americans, particularly those in western states, championed the war as a means to seize control of Canada. The war was also the result of a political showdown between the Democratic-Republican Party, which favored the conflict, and the Federalist

Party, which opposed the war. By labeling the Federalists' anti-war stance as unpatriotic, the Democratic-Republicans hoped to initiate a public backlash against the rival party and erode the Federalists' power in Washington, D.C.

The War of 1812 consumed the Madison administration for the next two years. It also left the U.S. military overstretched, which weakened the president's enthusiasm for committing soldiers to the Patriot War. In addition, the war in East Florida was not going well for the Patriots. The Seminole Indians were angered by the presence of armed Americans in their lands. Even with the help of the Georgia and Tennessee militias, the Patriots had a hard time repelling the Seminole.

What really spelled doom for Madison's support of the Patriot War, however, was the press coverage of the East Florida invasion. In the United States and abroad, Madison's administration was attacked for this latest act of American aggression on Spanish-held territory. The United States Senate responded by voting down the House resolution that allowed Madison to annex East Florida. In the face of this opposition, Madison had little choice but to repudiate the Patriots. The president did not exactly condemn Mathews. Madison said that the elderly rebel had erred in his invasion of Florida, his judgment clouded by his "zeal to promote the welfare of his country."[2] Secretary of State James Monroe made an official apology to Spain. President Madison agreed to withdraw the U.S. troops from East Florida, but only after Spain agreed not to prosecute the rebels. The last U.S. soldiers left the region in May 1813.

FIGHTING THE CREEKS

Even without the federal government's support, however, the Patriot War continued for another year. A small group of Patriots simply refused to give up. They were few in number, but they still managed to wreak havoc. They destroyed houses, farms, and plantations, making off with whatever livestock and foodstuffs they could steal. By the end of their spree, the region was devastated. According to eyewitness Isaac Bronson, the failed rebels left the "whole inhabited part of the province [East Florida] . . . in a state of utter desolution and ruin."[3]

The Patriot War was a disaster for East Florida. Especially to the north, the region was left a lawless wasteland. Many settled farmers left the area, and raiders and pirates moved in to take their place. The Patriot War also stirred up a deep animosity between the Americans and the Seminole. Even when the Patriot movement was over, the ill will it generated continued to fester for a long time.

Helping to fuel the anger of the Seminole was the Creek War (1813–1814). This conflict began as a civil war between different factions within the large Creek Indian Confederacy. The more traditional faction (the Upper Creek, also known as the Red Sticks) opposed the non-American Indian intruders in their lands. The less traditional faction (the Lower Creek, also known as the White Sticks) was more willing to work with white leaders.

On August 30, 1813, the Upper Creek attacked Fort Mims, about 40 miles north of Mobile. During the siege of the fort, the Upper Creek killed about 400 American men, women, and children. After the Fort Mims massacre, the Tennessee legislature funded an army of militiamen and Lower Creek allies to attack the Upper Creek. The army was led by General Andrew Jackson. A former U.S. congressman and senator from Tennessee, the general was already well known for his brashness and confidence, which often bordered on arrogance. Jackson's violent campaign against the Upper Creek culminated on March 27, 1814, at the Battle of Horseshoe Bend, during which Jackson's troops killed more than 700 Upper Creek warriors.

As the Creek War came to an end, Jackson forced some Creek leaders to sign the punishing Treaty of Fort Jackson. The treaty called for all the Creek—both allies and enemies of the United States—to surrender 23 million acres of their territory in what is now the southeastern United States. The agreement was an egregious betrayal of the Lower Creek who had joined

During the Battle of Horseshoe Bend, Andrew Jackson and his forces trapped and killed more than 700 Creek warriors. With their forces almost wiped out, Creek leaders surrendered to Jackson and were forced to sign a treaty that transferred millions of acres of land to the U.S. government. *Above*, Andrew Jackson accepts the surrender of Chief William Weatherford after the Battle of Horseshoe Bend.

Jackson's army. Jackson cared little about their complaints, however. He argued that because his Creek allies had turned against their own people, he could not trust them; he therefore was justified in treating them as badly as he did his Creek enemies. The Treaty of Fort Jackson outraged many Creek from both factions. Large numbers of Creek flocked to Spanish Florida, hoping to escape not only from American settlers, but also from their own leaders.

A NEW NATIONAL HERO

In addition to the Patriot War and the Creek War, Floridians were drawn into the War of 1812, which pitted the United States against Great Britain. When the war began, the British seized

Pensacola, the capital of West Florida, to use it as a military base. By 1814, the British in Pensacola were planning attacks on Mobile, Baton Rouge, and New Orleans. If the British were able to take over strongholds in American-occupied West Florida and New Orleans, they were likely to return these areas to Spanish control, an unwelcome prospect to the United States.

Now charged with protecting the Gulf Coast, General Andrew Jackson got wind of the British plans. He led an army of regular soldiers, militiamen, and American Indian allies to the Spanish fort at Pensacola. On November 7, 1814, at Jackson's demand, the Spanish governor surrendered the fort, and the British withdrew from the town. When President Madison heard about Pensacola, he was far from pleased. Jackson's foray into Florida jeopardized the United States' already shaky relationship with Spain at a time when the United States, already at war with Great Britain, could hardly afford to get entangled in another war. Madison immediately wrote to Jackson and ordered him to leave Pensacola.

At the same time, American and British negotiators were meeting in Ghent, in present-day Belgium. Both sides were tired of their costly war. The negotiators carved out an agreement. Although it did not resolve any of the conflicts that originally had led to the fighting, the Treaty of Ghent, signed on December 24, 1814, did signal the end of the War of 1812.

In an era without telephones or telegraphs, however, news of the negotiations took months to reach the United States. In the meantime, British ships and soldiers descended on New Orleans. Jackson and his men were ordered to defend the city. On January 8, 1815, the American army confronted the British in the Battle of New Orleans. Fought two weeks after the war's official end, the battle was a surprise victory for the United States. Already a popular figure, Andrew Jackson was hailed as great war leader and hero.

The years between 1811 and 1815 were a convulsive period for the people of East and West Florida. During that time, their

ANDREW JACKSON
(1767–1845)

Leader of the Common People

The dominant political figure of early nineteenth-century America, Andrew Jackson was born in the backwoods of what is now South Carolina on March 15, 1767. He grew up in poverty, with little schooling. By the time he reached his teens, both of his parents were dead. As a young man, Jackson fought in the American Revolution (1775–1783). During that war he was captured by the British; for the rest of his life, he bore a scar from a saber wound inflicted by one of his guards.

After the Revolution, Jackson began to study law. He settled in Nashville, Tennessee, and developed a lucrative law practice. He also formed tight-knit relationships with other prominent men in the area. With their support, Jackson became the first Tennessean elected to serve in the House of Representatives. He then went on to become one of the state's senators. Jackson also served as a judge with the Tennessee Superior Court.

Rash and ruthless, Jackson had a habit of making enemies. In 1806, he killed a man in a duel after the man made an unflattering remark about Jackson's wife. Seven years later, Jackson was shot during a brawl with two Missouri politicians, Thomas Hart Benton and his brother, Jesse Benton.

During the War of 1812, Jackson was placed in charge of the Tennessee militia. He became nationally famous after leading a successful campaign against the Creek Indians in 1813 and 1814 and engineering a spectacular defeat of British troops at the Battle of New Orleans in 1815. Three years later, during a campaign

lands were involved in three separate but related conflicts. In the end, however, these contests changed little about West Florida. It remained officially part of the Spanish empire, while

against the Seminole Indians, Jackson invaded Spanish Florida. To his supporters, the invasion was an act of heroism necessary to protect southern Americans from the threat of Seminole attack. To his detractors, it was an illegal and unconstitutional act of aggression against a foreign power.

In 1824, Jackson made his first bid for the White House, but he lost the presidency to his rival John Quincy Adams. Four years later, Jackson's growing popularity allowed him to defeat Adams and win the presidency.

Jackson's eight years as president (1828–1836) often are cited as a pivotal period in American history. He was the first president to reach his position by appealing directly to ordinary voters. During his two administrations, the political climate of Washington also became more democratic, as less wealthy Americans from the western frontier were given more access to power than they had had before.

Both Jackson the man and Jackson the president inspired controversy, however. He fired many government workers and replaced them with his friends and supporters. He threatened to send federal troops into South Carolina when citizens there resisted paying a tariff levied by the U.S. government. And he vetoed a bill that would recharter the Bank of America, an action that earned him the angry scorn of the bank's supporters.

Following his second term as president, Jackson retired from politics. He spent the rest of his life at the Hermitage, his Tennessee estate. On June 8, 1845, after a long stretch of ill health that left him a near invalid, Jackson died at age 78.

still under American occupation. In contrast, in East Florida, these conflicts caused devastating and long-term changes. The Patriot War left the region a wasteland. The Creek War stirred up a simmering hatred between the Seminole and the Americans. The War of 1812 and the conflict with the Creek raised the national profile of Andrew Jackson, giving him more power in American politics than he had had before. These events also reinforced Jackson's sense that his future and that of the Floridas were deeply entwined.

The Fight
for Florida

As the War of 1812 came to an end, diplomatic relations
between the United States and Spain were reestablished.
In 1814, the Spanish king, Ferdinand VII, was restored to the
throne. Because of this, the United States was again willing to
enter into diplomatic talks with Spain, and the two countries
soon returned to the negotiating table. The renewed dialogue
focused on what was to be done with Spanish Florida.

The United States hoped that Spain would recognize that
its loss of East Florida was inevitable. Spain hoped that the
United States, vulnerable after the expensive and inconclusive
War of 1812, would be willing to make significant concessions
to gain official control over both Floridas. With both sides
overreaching, the talks quickly stalled.

No one was more frustrated than the Spanish negotiator,
Luis de Onís. In his meetings with Secretary of State James

Monroe, Onís demonstrated a keen understanding of the Florida situation. Unlike many Spanish officials, he saw the issue with a clear eye, unclouded by stubborn pride. The Spanish authorities, however, did not give Onís the latitude he needed to propose a deal that the Americans would consider.

THE ATTACK ON NEGRO FORT

As Onís and Monroe hashed out their countries' positions, tensions in East Florida were again on the rise. The Seminole and Creek in the region were still angry about the American attacks during the Patriot War and the Creek War. At the same time, Americans just across the border were incensed that the Spanish authorities were doing little to control East Florida's populations of American Indians and runaway slaves. The Americans focused their wrath on the people who lived in a fort on the Apalachicola River. The British had abandoned the fort when they evacuated Florida in the spring of 1815. By early 1816, about 300 former slaves and 25 Seminole and Choctaw Indians resided at what the Americans called Negro Fort. The fort was equipped with a large supply of weaponry, including 2,500 muskets. In addition, hundreds of black settlers lived in towns near the fort, making the area the largest slave refuge yet established in North America.

Slave owners in Georgia were worried about Negro Fort. General Andrew Jackson, now the head of the Southern Division of the U.S. Army, shared their concern. President Madison wrote to Jackson, telling him to do nothing that would stir up a conflict. The headstrong Jackson ignored the president and wrote a letter of his own to the Spanish governor, Mauricio de Zuñiga. Jackson threatened the governor, saying that if Zuñiga refused to do anything about Negro Fort, he would.

Zuñiga had good reason not to take any action, however. He wanted to maintain good relations with Florida's American Indian population, who no doubt would be outraged if their brethren at Negro Fort were attacked. At the same time, Zuñiga did not want to anger Jackson. Zuñiga claimed to Jackson that he, too, was concerned about the fort but had to wait for instructions from his superiors before he could do anything.

While Zuñiga stalled, Jackson found the excuse he needed to act. Someone at Negro Fort fired shots at an American supply ship as it navigated the Apalachicola River. Using the incident to justify an attack, Jackson ordered Major General Edmund P. Gaines to destroy the fort. On July 27, 1816, Gaines's army of American soldiers and Lower Creek advanced on Negro Fort. As they approached, the army and the fort's defenders exchanged cannon fire. One cannon shot fired by the Americans landed directly on the fort's supply of gunpowder, touching off an enormous explosion. People in Pensacola—about 100 miles away—claimed that they heard the fort explode. Most of the fort's residents were killed. Among the few survivors were the fort's leaders, a black man named Garson and a Choctaw Indian chief. Both men were murdered by the Americans' Creek allies.

Without authority from the American president or from Spain, Jackson had ordered a devastating attack within the borders of Spanish Florida. The powers in Washington, D.C., and the Spanish capital of Madrid decided, however, that the less that was said about the matter, the better. Neither Spain nor the United States wanted to antagonize the other side and threaten the ongoing diplomatic negotiations.

TENSIONS GROW

The destruction of Negro Fort did not do much to stem the tide of runaway slaves into Florida. It did, however, add to the growing hostility between Americans and American Indians along the border. The Americans in the region were certain that the Seminole would seek revenge by attacking American settlements.

Bandits from Georgia posed an even greater threat to the region. Working in small gangs, these men crossed into Florida to raid American Indian villages and capture runaway slaves to sell to American slave owners. After Negro Fort was destroyed, these outlaws felt safer than ever in Florida. They were convinced that the weak Spanish authorities would do nothing to stop them.

In November 1816, former secretary of state James Monroe was elected the fifth president of the United States. Even before he took office, Monroe began to correspond with Jackson—a clear indication of the general's growing political power. In one letter, Monroe addressed the issue of Florida, a topic that he knew well from his dealings with Onís. Monroe wrote with confidence that, as long as Americans continued to move into the region, it was just a matter of time before Florida became part of the United States. Perhaps with Florida in mind, Monroe appointed John Quincy Adams as his replacement as secretary of state. The son of former president John Adams, John Quincy Adams already had had a distinguished career as a diplomat in Europe and Russia.

In the meantime, to the surprise of few, the tensions in East Florida continued to build. One reason was the arrival of trader Alexander Arbuthnot. The Scot developed a close relationship with the Seminole, who told their new friend all about their ill treatment by the Georgians. Arbuthnot agreed to mediate between the Seminole and the Spanish authorities. On behalf of Chief Bowlegs of the Seminole, Arbuthnot wrote to José Coppinger, the Spanish governor of East Florida, to ask Coppinger to protect the tribe from American abuses.

In the eyes of the Americans, Arbuthnot was a hopeless meddler at best and an instigator of American Indian violence at worst. Major General Gaines described the trader as "one of those self-styled philanthropists, who have for a long time past contrived to foment a spirit of discord amongst the Indians."[1] Anger toward Arbuthnot and other British inhabitants of East Florida

As U.S. secretary of state, James Monroe (*above*) spent 18 months intensely negotiating with Luis de Onís, his Spanish counterpart, over the ownership of Florida. Soon after he was elected president, Monroe enlisted the help of Andrew Jackson, a war hero who had fought inside the Florida territories, and John Quincy Adams, a skilled diplomat.

only grew after the Seminole attacked the Garrett homestead in
Georgia on February 24, 1817. Rumors quickly spread that the
British were supplying the Florida American Indians with weap-
ons and gunpowder.

THE GREEN CROSS OF FLORIDA

Adding to the chaos in East Florida was a Scottish soldier of fortune named Gregor MacGregor. He landed on Amelia Island,
off the Florida coast, on June 29, 1817. Leading a force of 150
men, he easily took over the port at Fernandina. (Only one
shot was fired, and that was an accident.) MacGregor hoisted
a flag showing a green cross on a white field and declared the
town independent of Spanish rule. The Spanish were upset by
MacGregor's takeover of Fernandina. The military force stationed in St. Augustine, however, was far too small and weak to
confront MacGregor and his men.

Some leaders in Washington, D.C., saw MacGregor's seizure
of Amelia Island as an excuse to grab East Florida once and for
all. They remembered how the No Transfer Resolution of 1811
gave the American president the authority to take control of
the region if it ever fell into foreign hands. Everyone knew that
the 1811 resolution had referred to a British takeover of East
Florida. MacGregor was a Scot and therefore British, but he
certainly did not represent his country. He was an adventurer
out for his own personal gain.

By nature, President Monroe was cautious. He listened to
the argument that the No Transfer Resolution could be applied
in the MacGregor case. In the end, however, Monroe was not
willing, with such flimsy justification, to stick out his neck and
take advantage of MacGregor's bold land grab.

SEIZING AMELIA ISLAND

Running low on men and supplies, MacGregor gave up on
Amelia Island in September. Now a well-established colony of

GREGOR MACGREGOR
(1786–1845)

"Liberator" of East Florida's Amelia Island

In 1817, a man named Gregor MacGregor arrived on Amelia Island with an army of 150 men and declared the island off the Florida coast an independent nation. The event was just one episode in the exciting and sometimes strange life of this Scottish adventurer. MacGregor was born in 1786 in Edinburgh, Scotland. As a young man, he joined the Royal Navy. He also served in the armies of Spain and Portugal, and he later claimed, he earned the title "Sir."

In 1811, MacGregor traveled to Venezuela. At the time, Venezuela and other South American colonies were rebelling against Spanish rule. In the chaos of these Latin American independence movements, the ambitious and vain MacGregor saw an opportunity to gain power, riches, and notoriety.

Eventually, MacGregor was driven by force from Venezuela. He remained enthusiastic about independence movements, however—so much so, in fact, that he decided to start his own. He gathered a small army of Scotsmen, promising them that they would soon become free landowners in the Americas. He and his men then sailed to the coast of Florida. On June 29, 1817, they quickly overwhelmed the small Spanish force on Amelia Island. The next day, MacGregor made a grandiose proclamation, in which he insisted that he meant no harm to the island's inhabitants. "Peaceable inhabitants of Amelia!" he proclaimed. "Do not apprehend any danger or oppression from the troops which are now in possession of your Island. . . . Their first object will be to protect your rights; your property will be held sacred and inviolable; and every thing done to promote your real interests."* Despite his promises, MacGregor

(continues)

(continued)

lacked the men and supplies to sustain his little island empire. He abandoned it in less than three months.

By 1820, MacGregor was back in Scotland. There he announced that he was the *cacique* (leader) of the newly independent South American country of Poyais. He explained that he had returned to Scotland to secure funding for the country's government and to attract settlers to the area. Charismatic and colorful, MacGregor entertained England's elite with exciting tales of his adventures and descriptions of the wonderful land of Poyais. In 1822, he published a guidebook to Poyais, detailing its natural resources and the opportunities that awaited settlers there. His public-relations campaign quickly bore fruit. He began selling land rights in Poyais and secured a loan of £200,000 for the nation's government.

Several hundred settlers set out for Poyais. Many exchanged their savings for the new nation's currency, which MacGregor had had printed up in Scotland. When they arrived in South America after a grueling sea journey, the settlers made a horrifying discovery. There was no nation of Poyais. MacGregor had made the whole thing up. By the time the survivors of the trip returned to London, MacGregor had escaped to Paris, France. There he resumed his Poyais scheme. He eventually was arrested for fraud but was acquitted in court. MacGregor continued to sell pieces of Poyais until 1839, when he returned to Venezuela. He died there in 1845.

---

* *"Another View of Gregor MacGregor,"* Amelia Now *(Winter 2001).*
Available online at http://www.amelianow.com/winter01-gregor.htm.

thieves, the island came under the control of a French pirate named Luis Aury. Under Aury, the situation became even more chaotic. The island became a base for smugglers who were bringing illegal goods and slaves into the United States. The smugglers regularly harassed Spanish and American ships that dared to sail too close to the island.

By the end of October 1817, President Monroe met with the members of his cabinet to figure out what to do about Amelia Island. With the cabinet's encouragement, the president decided to send in the U.S. Army and Navy to drive the pirates, bandits, and smugglers away. On December 2, Monroe went public with his plan for a military campaign to seize the island. He told Congress that the island had become "a channel for the illicit introduction of slaves into the United States, an asylum for fugitive slaves from neighboring states, and a port of smuggling of every kind."[2] Three weeks later, American soldiers and sailors invaded the island.

The Spanish were pleased to see this base for piracy brought under military control. They grew alarmed, however, when Monroe made no move to withdraw his troops. Encouraged by Secretary of War John C. Calhoun and Secretary of State John Quincy Adams, the president resolved to keep a military presence on Amelia indefinitely. The Spanish did nothing to stop him—a further testament to Spain's increasingly weak hold on East Florida.

MASSACRE AT FOWLTOWN

As the drama on Amelia Island unfolded, Jackson's subordinate Major General Gaines stirred up some trouble of his own in East Florida. Like Jackson, Gaines was eager for any excuse to invade the region. Stationed at Fort Scott in Georgia, Gaines made a habit of harassing nearby American Indians. By doing so, he hoped to provoke a fight that he could broaden into a larger military campaign. Gaines especially took to pestering the residents of the American Indian village of Fowltown, which lay in American territory just north of the Florida border. The residents of Fowltown were Creek who had close cultural ties to the Florida Seminole.

Fowltown was located on lands that some Creek leaders had ceded to the United States in the Treaty of Fort Jackson. Gaines had orders to force the tribes to leave the ceded area. The people of Fowltown, however, had not been involved in the treaty negotiations. They did not recognize the United States as having any legitimate claim to their village or the land around it. On November 19, 1817, Gaines sent a message to Neamathla, Fowltown's leader. Gaines wanted to talk with him about his people's removal from the village. Neamathla sent back word that he had no intention of ever meeting with Gaines.

The next day, Gaines sent a force of 250 soldiers to Fowltown to capture Neamathla. The villagers first fought the soldiers but then ran into nearby swamps to evade their bullets. Gaines was furious. A few days later, he sent his army back to Fowltown, which by then had been abandoned by the people who had lived there. The soldiers burned the village to the ground.

The destruction of Fowltown brought the simmering anger of the region's people to the boiling point. On November 30, a band of Seminole got their revenge by attacking an American supply boat under the command of Lieutenant R.W. Scott. The Seminole slaughtered more than 40 passengers, including several women and children.

A NEW POLICY

Secretary of War John C. Calhoun received word of the Scott Massacre a few weeks later. Gaines's meddling notwithstanding, the official goal of the U.S. Army had been to try to maintain peace with the American Indians in the border region.

Now, however, Calhoun decided to reverse this policy. He gave Gaines new instructions, which led to the conflict now known as the First Seminole War (1817–1818). Calhoun told Gaines to punish the Seminole, even if he had to follow them into Spanish Florida to do it. Calhoun also made a point of cautioning Gaines to stay away from Spanish forts: Gaines's campaign was against the Seminoles, not against the Spanish.

At the end of December 1817, Calhoun wrote a letter to Andrew Jackson. In it, the secretary of war asked Jackson to take over the Seminole campaign. Calhoun did not explicitly tell Jackson to stay clear of the Spanish as he had in his letter to Gaines. Perhaps Calhoun assumed that Jackson would understand that the secretary's original orders to Gaines applied to Jackson as well. Perhaps, Calhoun, familiar with Jackson's belligerence toward the Spanish, was trying to suggest, subtly, that Jackson exert control not only over the Seminole, but also over all of East Florida.

A few days later, President Monroe also wrote to Jackson. Although cryptic, the president's letter seemed to offer Jackson even more encouragement to make the most of his invasion of Spanish Florida. "[M]ovement . . . against the Seminoles . . . will bring you on a theatre where you may possibly have other services to perform," the president wrote. "Great interests are at issue. . . . This is not a time for repose . . . until our cause is carried triumphantly thro."[3]

Historians still argue about whether or not Monroe knowingly was instructing Jackson to battle the Spanish and seize East Florida. It is clear, however, that that was precisely the message that Jackson heard. Before beginning the campaign, Jackson took a moment to write to Monroe about what he hoped to do:

[T]he whole of East Florida [should be] seized and held as an indemnity for the outrages of Spain upon the property of

In response to the Scott Massacre, Secretary of War John C. Calhoun
initially warned the U.S. military to avoid Spanish forts while pursuing
the perpetrators of the attack in Florida. Aware that President James
Monroe wanted the Florida territories, Calhoun then enlisted Andrew
Jackson—a pugnacious, hotheaded general—to take charge of the
campaign, but without issuing any caution against antagonizing Spanish officials.

our citizens; this done, it puts all opposition down, secures to our citizens a complete indemnity, and saves us from a war with Spain. This can be done without implicating the government; let it be signified to me through any channel ... that the possession of the Floridas would be desirable ... and in sixty days it will be accomplished.[4]

An Illegal War?

Andrew Jackson led his men across the border into Spanish Florida on March 12, 1818. For weeks, they wandered the region, looking, with limited success, for Seminole Indians to fight. Then, on April 6, Jackson took the initiative to attack a second enemy—the Spanish authorities at the fort of St. Marks. At St. Marks, Jackson discovered the Scottish trader Alexander Arbuthnot, whom he blamed, improbably, for fanning the Seminole's hostility toward American settlers. After a mock trial, Jackson ordered the execution of Arbuthnot and another British captive, adventurer Robert Christie Ambrister.

Jackson wrote to Secretary of War John C. Calhoun to declare that his war against the Seminole was now over, and he was disbanding his army. Jackson soon had a change of heart, however. He decided to continue his campaign against the Spanish in Florida. On May 5, Jackson drafted another letter to Calhoun, in which he explained his new mission. The general wrote that he was heading to Pensacola, the capital of West Florida. Jackson insisted that there were between 400 and 500 American Indians at the fort who were receiving aid and weapons from the Spanish. Jackson held that, if these American Indians were not subdued, they were sure to attack settlers in what is now southern Alabama.

As Jackson prepared to do battle at Pensacola, he received a disturbing report. A group of militiamen from Georgia had descended on the Creek village of Chehaw. With their swords, the Georgians had hacked to death dozens of Creek, mostly women and children, and then set the village on fire. Most of the men of Chehaw had been away from the village at the time. They were allies of Jackson and were helping the American general to fight his bitter war against the Seminole. The Chehaw tragedy showed starkly that all tribes—whether friends or foes of the Americans—were victimized by the anti-American Indian hysteria that Jackson himself had done his best to spread throughout the borderlands.

ON TO PENSACOLA

Leaving a small force at St. Marks, Jackson led about 1,000 men toward the West Florida capital. Without adequate maps, they had trouble finding their way. They got lost and wandered aimlessly for nearly two weeks before getting their bearings.

As the American army made its slow approach, the Spanish governor at Pensacola, José Masot, tired to figure out what to do. He decided to draft a letter to Jackson to dissuade the general from attacking the town. In his letter, Masot explained that he was not harboring hostile American Indians. There were a few American Indians in town, but nowhere near the 500 that Jackson claimed were there. (The total population of Pensacola at the time was only about 400.) Masot also assured Jackson that his men were not blocking American supply ships, another accusation leveled by the U.S. general.

JACKSON AT PENSACOLA.

Andrew Jackson claimed there was a large population of American Indians in Pensacola, a Florida town. After two weeks of trekking through the wilderness, Jackson and his men *(above)* finally arrived to find that the Spanish governor, José Masot, had deserted the city in fear of Jackson and his troops.

Ignoring the Spaniard's letter, Jackson and his army continued their laborious advance on Pensacola. Masot tried again, this time writing to Jackson with a threat of violence if his force did not withdraw at once. Undaunted, the Americans kept heading for the town. Masot finally took action, but instead of attacking Jackson's force, he withdrew his own men from Pensacola and retreated to nearby Fort San Carlos de Barrancas. On May 23, Jackson took control of a deserted Pensacola.

Jackson still had some more fight in him. He demanded that Masot give up Barrancas as well. When Masot refused, Jackson prepared for battle. Leaving behind about 150 troops to secure Pensacola, Jackson led the rest of his force to Barrancas. Outnumbered, the Spanish there could not resist the attack. On May 28, as American cannon fire pounded the fort, Masot surrendered. At Masot's request, Jackson deported him and his men, sending them to the Spanish colony of Cuba. Jackson then declared that one of his officers, Colonel William King, was the provisional governor of all of Spanish Florida. According to Jackson, the entire area was now under American rule.

NEWS REACHES WASHINGTON

Throughout the spring of 1818, reports about what was happening in Spanish Florida trickled into Washington. On May 4, President Monroe learned of Jackson's seizure of the fort at St. Marks. The news was troubling. Suddenly, Monroe found himself having to explain away an unauthorized attack on a Spanish fort in Spanish territory. After meeting with his cabinet, Monroe decided to play down the incident. He pretended that it was just an extension of his policy toward Amelia Island—that is, American troops had stepped in to restore order and would stay just until the Spanish were able to secure the post.

The bad news kept coming. The president soon learned about Arbuthnot and Ambrister. Monroe worried about how the British would react to the execution of two of their citizens by an American general without a proper trial. Then the president found out about the Chehaw massacre. He feared that this atrocity, committed by American militiaman, could cause the entire southern frontier to explode into violence.

Worst of all, however, was the news about Jackson's takeover of Pensacola—an event that Monroe first learned of from the newspapers. The president had no idea about how to respond to this unprovoked attack on the Spanish capital. Deciding to dodge the press, Monroe fled to his farm in Virginia. He left Secretary of State John Quincy Adams to deal with the growing controversy.

ADAMS TAKES A STAND

Adams took a careful look at the situation and weighed the pros and cons of lending the administration's support to Jackson's actions. On one hand, what Jackson had done was in flagrant violation of the U.S. Constitution. The Constitution states that only Congress has the authority to declare war against a foreign power. Clearly, even if Jackson had been encouraged by the president to overstep his bounds, the general did not have the approval of Congress to take over Spanish Florida in the name of the United States. Henry Clay, the speaker of the House of Representatives, already was railing against Jackson's outrageous power grab. A powerful politician and a brilliant orator, Clay made the case to his fellow Congressmen that Jackson needed to be punished for his illegal acts.

On the other hand, Adams also saw that Jackson had plenty of supporters. Many Americans, especially in the South, considered Jackson a national hero. Whatever he did, right or wrong, he had their backing. In addition, Americans generally were pleased by the Florida invasion. In their eyes, Jackson was fighting Indians and claiming Spanish territory on America's behalf. To many people, these ends justified the means. They were not interested in interpreting the Constitution or in debating American treaty obligations to American Indians and foreigners. What they cared about was getting their hands on fertile Florida lands.

John Quincy Adams also came to recognize that Jackson's actions could benefit Adams personally. If Adams was to be a success as secretary of state, he had to find a way to make Spanish Florida part of the United States. Jackson had just made that job far easier. With U.S. troops holding Florida, it was clear that Spain had no hope of hanging on to this territory. Jackson's invasion had greatly strengthened Adams's bargaining position in his ongoing negotiations with Spanish diplomat Luis de Onís.

For Adams, that was enough to tip the balance. In his public life, he was a vigorous defender of the U.S. Constitution,

Andrew Jackson's brazen takeover of Florida incited outrage among some politicians in Washington, D.C., who accused the general of breaking the law by invading foreign territory. Secretary of State John Quincy Adams *(above)*, did not agree with Jackson's military actions, but supported the general in order to further the process of acquiring new territory.

which his beloved father, John Adams, had helped to draft. In the end, however, Adams was willing to ignore Jackson's disregard for the law of the land if doing so would help bring Florida into American hands.

MULLING OVER THE FLORIDA SITUATION

Monroe was less certain about what to do. Congress was adjourned for the summer, but when it came back into session, Monroe knew that its members would be asking plenty of questions about Florida. Soon, he would have to make a public statement about Jackson and Florida. He was not sure what to say. Back in Washington in mid-July, Monroe called his cabinet together to help him formulate a Florida policy.

In the cabinet meeting, Adams and Calhoun dominated the discussion. Adams insisted that the president stand by Jackson. The secretary of state said that, given the situation, the general was completely justified in his actions. Just as adamantly, Secretary of War Calhoun argued that Monroe could not simply ignore what Jackson had done. The general had violated the Constitution, insisted Calhoun, and he should be court-martialed.

Both secretaries had ulterior motives for their arguments regarding Jackson. Adams wanted Jackson exonerated because such a move would put Adams in a better position in his negotiations with Onís. Calhoun wanted to see Jackson humiliated because he considered the general his greatest political rival.

Monroe wavered back and forth. He knew that if he supported Jackson, he would be attacked by Congress for stripping away its war-making powers. If he punished Jackson, he would invite the wrath of the general's many supporters. In the end, Monroe decided on a middle-of-the-road approach. The president would not condemn Jackson personally. He would hold, however, that Jackson's actions were not in line with official U.S. policy. Monroe also decided to return Pensacola and St. Marks to Spanish control.

Secretary of War Calhoun wrote to Major General Gaines, who was still in Florida, about the plan to pull U.S. troops from the Spanish posts. This news upset both Gaines and Jackson. Far from retreating from Florida, they wanted to expand their mission by attacking St. Augustine. Again, the two military men exaggerated the American Indian threat in Florida. They claimed that a large Seminole force was poised to strike St. Augustine if American soldiers did not stop it. Calhoun did not accept their argument. He wrote to Gaines to telling him, point-blank, that he was to fight no one unless he was attacked first. The cabinet was busily trying to think of some way to excuse Jackson for his behavior in Florida. The last thing it needed was another act of American aggression to justify.

SPAIN REACTS

As the cabinet strategized, Luis de Onís got wind of what Jackson had done in Florida. Furious, he headed to Washington and fired off an angry letter to Adams. On Onís's orders, the messenger woke Adams in the middle of the night to deliver the note. With some justification, Onís wrote, "the war against the Seminoles has been merely a pretext for General Jackson to fall, as a conqueror, upon the Spanish provinces . . . for the purpose of establishing there the dominion of this republic upon the odious basis of violence and bloodshed."[1] Onís demanded that the administration disavow Jackson's actions.

Spain reacted to the news from Florida by breaking off all diplomatic relations with the United States. Spanish officials felt obliged to take a strong stance on the issue. It is also likely that they wanted to see what the international reaction would be. The Spanish hoped that the British would come to their defense. With a powerful ally supporting Spain, the United States would be at a disadvantage in any future talks about Florida's fate.

Even after the executions of Arbuthnot and Ambrister, however, Great Britain was not interested in getting involved in the Florida issue. Worse for Spain, British diplomats were engaged in talks with Secretary of State Adams to resolve outstanding disputes that had not been settled by the War of 1812. The result was the Convention of 1818, an agreement that dealt mainly with fishing rights and boundaries in the Pacific Northwest. This document, signed on October 20, 1818, demonstrated that the United States and Great Britain now were on friendly terms. It was clear that Spain could not expect Great Britain to jeopardize this situation by siding with Spain in the Florida controversy.

In the fall of 1818, Spain decided to restore diplomatic relations with the United States. In truth, Spain had little choice in the matter. The Spanish government was in a financial crisis. It did not have enough economic and military resources to fight the United States for Florida, especially with U.S. troops already occupying the area. The Spanish feared, with those troops nearby, that Americans might try to take over Spanish-held Texas. To add to Spain's troubles, other Spanish-controlled territories in Central and South America, such as Argentina and Chile, were in revolt. Afraid of losing all of its land in the Americas, Spain needed to negotiate with the United States to ensure that Washington would not officially recognize these rebel governments.

As Luis de Onís returned to the negotiation table, one thing was clear. Onís knew, as did Adams, that it was unlikely, now, that Spain would be able to keep its hold on Florida. For Onís, the situation posed a challenge. Although he was in a weak bargaining position, Onís had to find a way to cede Florida to the United States on the best possible terms for Spain.

The Florida
Controversy

As their renewed negotiations began, both Adams and Onís agreed on one thing: The two Floridas were to become part of the United States. Exactly what Spain would get in return for this land cession was a matter of dispute, however. It soon became clear that the outcome would hinge on the negotiation of a clearer border between American and Spanish lands.

Ever since the Louisiana Purchase in 1803, the boundary between Spanish and American territories in North America had been uncertain. For years, Spain had argued that the Mississippi River was the western border of the United States. Because this border placed most of the Louisiana Purchase in Spanish hands, the United States hotly disputed the claim.

In past negotiations, Adams had made a case for a border along the Rocky Mountains. Now that the Florida issue had given him a bargaining advantage, Adams made a bold move.

He proposed a border that extended American territory all the way to the Pacific Ocean. Onís resisted the idea. As the talks continued, though, it became clear that Spain might consider a transcontinental border (a border that would allow the United States to stretch across the North American continent) if the United States would guarantee Spanish control over Texas.

INVESTIGATING JACKSON

While Adams and Onís haggled, Washington was drawn into another controversy. In late 1818, Congress prepared for a formal investigation of Jackson's invasion of Florida. In the House of Representatives, the military affairs committee would examine the executions of Arbuthnot and Ambrister, and the foreign relations committee would study the war's repercussions on the United States's relations with Spain.

Newspapers were filled with stories about Florida, and congressmen began to line up on both sides of the issue. Some congressmen were vehement Jackson supporters who demanded that he be cleared of any wrongdoing. Others spoke out emotionally against the general's impulsive and illegal behavior. Many members of Congress were political rivals of Jackson or of Monroe; these men saw in the controversy a chance to discredit their enemies while advancing their own careers.

Jackson was outraged that anyone was questioning his actions at all. Even so, he prepared to defend himself. In his defense, Jackson focused on his seizure of Pensacola. He wanted to prove that the Spanish there had harbored hundreds of hostile Seminole, thus making his takeover a military necessity. On Jackson's orders, an associate traveled to Florida to get signed affidavits from eyewitnesses, testifying that there was a large Indian population at the Spanish town.

Jackson also called on his friend William Hambly, a former soldier in his army, to come to Washington to swear that he had heard from reliable sources that about 500 Seminole fled from Pensacola when they learned that Jackson's army was approaching. Soon, Jackson also claimed that Spanish governor José Masot was personally responsible for blocking American supply ships, thereby providing further justification for the Americans' attack. Jackson remarked that his only regret about his mission in Florida was that he had not hanged Masot when he had the chance.

JOHN QUINCY ADAMS
(1767–1848)

First Son and President

John Quincy Adams was the sixth president of the United States. Today, however, he is more well regarded for his skill as a diplomat and a congressman than for any achievements he made during his tenure in the White House. Born on July 11, 1767, Adams was a native of Massachusetts. During John Quincy's boyhood, his father, John Adams, was an important leader of the American Revolution (1775–1783). The elder Adams later became the second president of the United States. Young John Quincy accompanied his father on several trips to Europe. At 14, during the American Revolution, he also traveled to Russia as the private secretary of American diplomat Francis Dana.

Following the Revolution, John Quincy Adams returned to Massachusetts to study law. After completing his studies, he embarked on a diplomatic career and represented the United States in several countries in Europe. On his return to the United States, he gave up diplomacy for politics. In 1803, he was elected to the U.S. Senate. In 1808, frustrated by President Thomas Jefferson's trade policies, he resigned.

After carrying out diplomatic missions to Russia and Great Britain, Adams was appointed secretary of state by President James

(continues)

(continued)

Monroe. In this position, Adams negotiated the Transcontinental Treaty of 1819, which gave the United States control over Florida and set the country's western boundary at the Pacific Ocean. He also was the architect of the Monroe Doctrine, which held that the United States would not accept any future colonization of North America by European nations.

Adams ran for the presidency in 1824. His opponent, Andrew Jackson, received the most electoral votes. No candidate won a majority of electoral votes, however, so the House of Representatives decided the election. With the support of Speaker of the House Henry Clay, Adams won the presidency.

Throughout Adams's four years in office, he endured constant attacks from Jackson supporters who claimed that he stole the election. With little support in Washington, Adams was not able to get much done. In 1828, when he ran for a second term, Jackson defeated him.

After a brief retirement, Adams ran for the House of Representatives. He won a seat in 1830. In Congress, he fought hard against the expansion of slavery. He also championed the cause of a group of African slaves who had staged a mutiny on a ship called the *Amistad*. Representing the Africans before the U.S. Supreme Court, Adams helped win them their freedom in the United States.

Adams also opposed the Mexican-American War (1846–1848). As he spoke out against the war on the floor of the House, he suffered a massive stroke. Too ill to be moved, the ailing Adams remained in the U.S. Capitol. There, he died two days later, on February 23, 1848.

MONROE TRIES TO HELP

Monroe found Jackson's attempts at self-justification exhausting. It was fairly obvious that Jackson's claims about large numbers of armed American Indians at Pensacola were a fabrication.

One of the youngest members of Congress in U.S. history, Senator John Eaton was good friends with Andrew Jackson and supported the general in the Florida controversy. Advising Jackson to refrain from confronting his accusers, Eaton helped the general save his political career. After Jackson was elected president, he returned the favor by appointing Eaton as his secretary of war.

Perhaps worse, his claims were irrelevant to the charges being leveled at him. Jackson was a man who often did whatever he wanted without fully considering the consequences, and he seemed unable to understand the seriousness of his situation. Jackson offered no defense at all against the assertion that his conduct had subverted the war-making powers granted to Congress by the Constitution.

Monroe tried to persuade Jackson to take a different tack to protect himself. The president wanted Jackson to say publicly that he had misunderstood his orders. Monroe also suggested, subtly, that Jackson alter some of his earlier reports to exaggerate wrongdoing on the part of the Spanish in Florida. Jackson refused both requests. He insisted to the president that he had understood his orders perfectly and that he had done nothing wrong.

The more attention the Florida controversy attracted, the more agitated Jackson became. In December 1817, newspapers reported rumors that Jackson was heading to Washington, D.C., to confront his detractors in person. Disturbed by these accounts, Senator John Eaton, a close friend of Jackson's, wrote to the general from the capital, urging him to stay put in Tennessee. Eaton knew Jackson well enough to fear that if he came to Washington, he somehow would get himself into even more trouble.

THE ERVING LETTER

Secretary of State Adams spent the Christmas season agonizing over a letter that he was writing to George Erving, an American diplomat in Madrid, Spain. The letter was meant to instruct Erving how to present the Monroe administration's stance on the Florida invasion to the governments of Europe. Adams knew, however, that the letter would be published and read widely, both abroad and at home. It therefore represented Adams's best opportunity to explain to the American public that the United States was justified in seizing Florida and that Jackson was innocent of any crime.

For three weeks, Adams worked on his letter to Erving. He carefully crafted not only an argument, but also a narrative—a story that portrayed Americans in Florida as a force for good and depicted the Spanish, the British, and the Seminole there as forces for evil. In detailing the events leading up to the invasion, Adams left out anything that made the Americans look bad. He described Seminole attacks on settlers and soldiers, but he did not mention Jackson's betrayal of his Creek allies with the Treaty of Fort Jackson or Gaines's unwarranted destruction of Fowltown. Adams claimed that Alexander Arbuthnot was completely to blame for the hostilities between the Americans and the Seminole. Furthermore, the secretary of state maintained, the old trader was part of a conspiracy that sought to incite the Seminole to wage a "savage, servile, exterminating war against the United States."[1]

In the letter, Adams also held that Jackson was completely in the right in everything he did. The general had seized St. Marks and Pensacola "not in the spirit of hostility to Spain, but as necessary measures of self-defense."[2] According to Adams, because Jackson was motivated only by the "purest patriotism,"[3] there was no reason for the president to punish or rebuke the general.

Adams did recommend some further investigation into the Florida matter—not into Jackson's actions, but into those of the local Spanish officials. Adams said that Spain needed to look into whether those officials actively assisted hostile American Indians. In a particularly bold stroke, Adams went so far as to say that Spain should compensate the United States for the cost of the American invasion because the invading Americans had tried to protect the people of Florida after the Spanish authorities had proved that they were not up to the task.

GUIDING THE DEBATE

Some of Adams's assertions were exaggerations. Others were almost absurd. When all was said and done, however, the Erving letter had exactly the effect that its author had hoped for. After its publication in the United States, on December 28, 1818, the Erving letter reframed the debate on Florida and helped Jackson's defenders to make their case. To those already inclined to like Jackson, Adams's take on the Florida invasion was pleasing and comforting. It allowed them to put aside any qualms they might have had about the illegality of the war, and it encouraged them to embrace the notion that Jackson was simply a noble patriot fighting off an evil, foreign foe of the United States. The letter also gave Jackson's friends additional ammunition to use against the general's detractors. According to the argument set out by Adams, anyone who criticized Jackson could be painted as pro-Spanish or, even worse, anti-American.

Adams had laid out the best case for Jackson that he could. He still was nervous about the congressional investigations, however. On January 12, 1819, when the House Committee on Military Affairs released its report, it was clear that Adams had good reason to be concerned. Confined to a study of the executions of Arbuthnot and Ambrister, the report was extremely critical of Jackson. It stated explicitly that Jackson's seizure of St. Marks and Pensacola was "contrary to orders and in violation of the constitution."[4] The findings of the committee were strongly influenced by Secretary of the Treasury William Crawford, who had a long-standing feud with Jackson.

As a result of the committee's report, Georgia congressman Thomas W. Cobb introduced three resolutions calling for new legislation to be considered by the House of Representatives. The first resolution proposed barring the execution of war prisoners without the permission of the president. The second sought to prohibit the invasion of foreign territory without congressional approval. The third called for an official disapproval of the seizure of St. Marks and Pensacola, citing it as a violation of the U.S. Constitution.

REBUKING JACKSON

The members of the House of Representatives soon began to debate the three resolutions. For 26 days, they hashed out just about every aspect of the Florida controversy. At the heart of

(continues on page 80)

Henry Clay, a powerful politician, sought to destroy the reputations of Andrew Jackson and President James Monroe during the Florida controversy. Described by Jackson as "the basest, meanest, scoundrel that ever disgraced the image of his god," Clay had enormous clout in Congress and did his best to hurt Jackson's political ambitions.

HENRY CLAY ON THE FLORIDA CONTROVERSY

During the 1819 investigation into General Andrew Jackson's conduct in Florida, dozens of congressmen spoke out, either in favor of the general or against him. Day after day, the galleries of the House of Representatives were filled with spectators. The crowds were particularly excited to hear from Speaker of the House Henry Clay of Kentucky. If any congressman was bound to deliver some explosive rhetoric, it was the fiery Clay.

By 1819, Henry Clay already had had an exalted career in Congress, having served numerous terms in both the Senate and the House. A successful lawyer before entering politics, Clay was a charismatic figure. Charming, temperamental, and extraordinarily ambitious, he had a great reputation for stirring oratory. With an eye toward eventually reaching the White House, Clay had coveted the job of secretary of state in the administration of President James Monroe. He was infuriated when the president instead gave the post to John Quincy Adams. For Clay, the Florida investigation offered a perfect opportunity. He could attack Jackson, a political rival, and at the same subtly jab at Monroe and Adams.

In this excerpt from Clay's speech on the Florida affair, the congressman argues that, if the House leaves Jackson's insubordination unpunished, it will be an embarrassment to the nation and a defeat for all defenders of the U.S. Constitution.

We are fighting a great moral battle for the benefit not only of our country, but of all mankind. The eyes of the whole world are in fixed attention upon us. . . . When the minions of despotism heard, in Europe, of the seizure of Pensacola, how did they chuckle, and chide the admirers of our institutions, tauntingly pointing to the

demonstration of a spirit of injustice and aggrandizement made by our country, in the midst of an amicable negotiation! Behold, said they, the conduct of those who are constantly reproaching kings! You saw how those admirers were astounded and hung their heads. . . . Beware how you give a fatal sanction, in this infant period of our Republic, scarcely yet twoscore years old, to military insubordination. . . .

Are [General Jackson's] former services, however eminent, to preclude even inquiry into recent misconduct? Is there to be no limit, no prudential bounds to the national gratitude? I am not disposed to censure the President for not ordering a court of inquiry, or a general court-martial. Perhaps, impelled by a sense of gratitude, he determined, by anticipation, to extend to the general that pardon which he had the undoubted right to grant after sentence. Let us not shrink from our duty. Let us assert our constitutional powers, and vindicate the instrument from military violation.

I hope gentlemen will deliberately survey the awful isthmus on which we stand. [Jackson's supporters] may bear down all opposition; they may even vote the general the public thanks; they may carry him triumphantly through this House. But, if they do, in my humble judgment, it will be a triumph of the principle of insubordination, a triumph of the military over the civil authority, a triumph over the powers of this House, a triumph over the Constitution of the land. And I pray most devoutly to Heaven that it may not prove, in its ultimate effects and consequences, a triumph over the liberties of the people.*

*Daniel Mallory, ed., The Life and Speeches of the Hon. Henry Clay, Volume 1. New York: Robert P. Bixby & Co., 1843, pp. 388–389.

(continued from page 77)

the discussion, however, was one central question: Did Jackson violate the Constitution by deciding, on his own, to attack the Spanish in Florida?

The most anticipated speech was the one delivered by Henry Clay. The powerful Speaker of the House intensely disliked both Jackson and Monroe, and this speech gave him a golden opportunity to damage two of his biggest political enemies. Ironically, Clay had been a vocal supporter of the occupation of West Florida. Now, he had little trouble switching positions and condemning Jackson's Florida land grab if doing so meant that he could score a serious blow against the popular general.

Clay previously had shown little sympathy for beleaguered Indian peoples. In his speech, however, he railed against Jackson for his ill-treatment of the Seminole. Clay's fellow congressmen surely could smell the opportunism in this sudden change of heart. As New York senator Rufus King remarked, "I cannot join in the hue and cry with them, who with altogether different motives, are zealously, and for the first time in their lives, the champions of humanity, the teachers of the milder virtues, the accusers of the vindictive white warrior, and the protectors of the red men."[5] Clay was on more solid ground when he spoke about the unconstitutionality of the invasion. He asked his audience to look with clarity at Jackson's challenge to congressional authority, no matter what their personal feelings might be for the hero of the Battle of New Orleans. Clay asked, "Are former services, however eminent, to protect from even inquiring into recent misconduct?"[6]

HERO OR HOTHEAD?

As eloquent as Clay was, his argument was unpersuasive for many of his listeners. They were not eager to view Jackson as a brutalizer of innocent American Indians and a hotheaded warmonger with no regard for the rule of law. They much preferred the Jackson presented by Adams in the Erving letter—the stalwart warrior, willing to do battle against scheming foreigners and their bloodthirsty American Indian allies who together were determined to destroy the American way of life.

Seen as a war hero who saved the United States from the dangerous Spanish and American Indian forces, most of the U.S. public supported Andrew Jackson's actions in Florida. *Above*, Jackson celebrates after being promoted to major general following his victory at the Battle of Horseshoe Bend.

In addition, Jackson's violation of the Constitution seemed a fairly abstract idea to many of his supporters. It seemed unfair that this hero should be punished because different branches of the government were squabbling over which had authority over what. At the same time, Jackson's actions had resulted in a concrete benefit: Florida now was in American hands. Even those Jackson supporters who understood the seriousness of the constitutional issue were willing to look the other way because Jackson had delivered such a wonderful prize to the United States.

All of this goodwill toward Jackson was threatened, however, when the general arrived in Washington during the House debates. His friends implored him to stay calm. They feared that he would sound off in public and thereby lend credence to Clay's portrayal of him as reckless and arrogant. Generally, Jackson behaved himself; in private, however, he made physical threats against his opponents. He grumbled that as soon as the congressional session was over, he would challenge Clay to a duel. Jackson even threatened to slice off the ears of one senator who annoyed him.

CONGRESS VINDICATES THE GENERAL

On February 8, 1819, the U.S. Army formally returned control of Pensacola to Spain. On the same day, the House of Representatives held a vote on the resolutions concerning the Florida controversy. By large margins, the House voted down all three. The votes were an enormous victory for Jackson. Vindicated of all wrongdoing, he set off on a tour of New England. Wherever he went, he was treated to parades and banquets in his honor.

Three weeks after the House vote, the Senate issued a report on its own investigation into Florida. The Senate's findings were a scathing indictment of Jackson. In no uncertain terms, the report stated that the general had ignored orders and subverted the authority of the president and Congress. It further asserted that his actions amounted to "a wound on the national character."[7]

As incendiary as its conclusions were, the Senate report was swept quickly under the rug. It never was debated in Congress, and it was virtually ignored everywhere else in Washington. The powers in the nation's capital had already made a political calculation. Although Jackson had ignored the laws of the land, he would be celebrated rather than condemned. For the United States, Florida finally was within reach. It was ripe for the taking, and nothing else seemed to matter.

Coming to an Agreement

Like most people in Washington, Luis de Onís closely followed the House investigation into the Florida invasion. When the investigation ended with the total vindication of Jackson, Onís became worried about his negotiations with Adams. It was clear that the U.S. government was happy to throw principle aside if doing so improved its chances of annexing Florida. It was as though the elites in Washington had decided that rules about international boundaries no longer applied to American lawmakers. With that mindset, what would stop the United States from trying to grab other Spanish-held territories that Spain was in no position to defend?

In the weeks that followed, Onís and Adams worked on their treaty. Adams aggressively sought a transcontinental boundary and strove to carve out as large a swath of land as possible bordering on the Pacific Ocean. Onís concentrated on

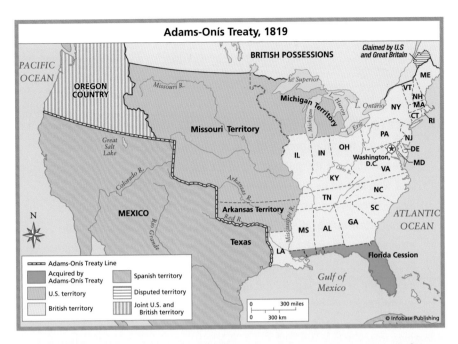

The Adams-Onís Treaty, named after Secretary of State John Quincy Adams and Spanish foreign minister Luis de Onís, finalized the transfer of ownership of Florida from Spain to the United States. The treaty also finally established a mutually agreed-upon international boundary separating American and Spanish territory in North America.

securing Spain's claim to Texas. Given the circumstances, he determined that this was the most Spain could hope to get from the United States.

SIGNING THE TREATY

On February 20, 1819, Adams and Onís finally reached an agreement. At Adams's request, they waited until February 22—the birthday of Founding Father George Washington—to sign the document. This served to underscore the importance of the event. Formally called the Treaty of Amity, Settlement, and Limits Between the United States of America and His Catholic Majesty, the agreement also was known as the Transcontinental

(continues on page 88)

THE TRANSCONTINENTAL TREATY OF 1819

In 1819, after many years of negotiation, Secretary of State John Quincy Adams and Spanish diplomat Luis de Onís finally reached an agreement about the possession of East and West Florida. The treaty that was signed by the two men on February 22, 1819, required Spain to cede the territory of East Florida to the United States. The Spanish territory of West Florida had been occupied by American troops since 1810. By establishing that West Florida was American territory, the 1819 treaty legitimized this occupation and formalized the United States's legally dubious possession of the region. This excerpt from the treaty lists the primary concessions made by the United States and Spain to complete the transfer of the Floridas.

The United States of America and His Catholic Majesty, desiring to consolidate, on a permanent basis, the friendship and good correspondence which happily prevails between the two parties, have determined to settle and terminate all their differences and pretensions, by a treaty, which shall designate, with precision, the limits of their respective bordering territories in North America. . . .

There shall be a firm and inviolable peace and sincere friendship between the United States and their citizens and His Catholic Majesty, his successors and subjects, without exception of persons or places.

His Catholic Majesty cedes to the United States, in full property and sovereignty, all the territories which belong to him, situated to the eastward of the Mississippi, known by the name of East and West Florida. . . .

The boundary-line between the two countries, west of the Mississippi, shall begin on the Gulph of Mexico, at the mouth of

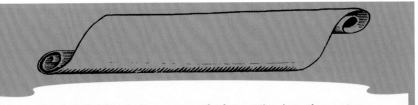

the river Sabine, in the sea, continuing north, along the western bank of that river, to the 32d degree of latitude; . . .

The inhabitants of the ceded territories shall be secured in the free exercise of their religion, without any restriction; and all those who may desire to remove to the Spanish dominions shall be permitted to sell or export their effects, at any time whatever, without being subject, in either case, to duties.

The inhabitants of the territories which His Catholic Majesty cedes to the United States, by this treaty, shall be incorporated in the Union of the United States as soon as may be consistent with the principles of the Federal Constitution. . . .

The officers and troops of His Catholic Majesty, in the territories hereby ceded by him to the United States, shall be withdrawn. . . .

All grants made since the said 24th of January, 1818, when the first proposal, on the part of His Catholic Majesty, for the cession of the Floridas was made, are hereby declared and agreed to be null and void. . . .

The United States, exonerating Spain from all demands in future, on account of the claims of their citizens to which the renunciations herein contained extend, and considering them entirely cancelled, undertake to make satisfaction for the same, to an amount not exceeding five millions of dollars. . . .

In witness whereof we, the underwritten Plenipotentiaries of the United States of America and of His Catholic Majesty, have signed, by virtue of our powers, the present treaty of amity,

(continues)

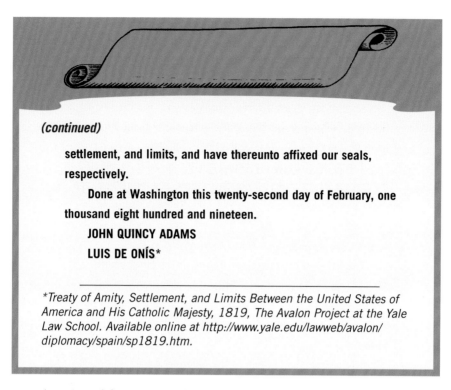

(continued)

settlement, and limits, and have thereunto affixed our seals, respectively.

Done at Washington this twenty-second day of February, one thousand eight hundred and nineteen.

JOHN QUINCY ADAMS

LUIS DE ONÍS*

---

*Treaty of Amity, Settlement, and Limits Between the United States of America and His Catholic Majesty, 1819, The Avalon Project at the Yale Law School. Available online at http://www.yale.edu/lawweb/avalon/diplomacy/spain/sp1819.htm.

(continued from page 85)

Treaty of 1819 or, popularly, the Adams-Onís Treaty. It gave the United States authority over East Florida and formally recognized American control over West Florida. Spain received no direct payment for the land cession. The United States did agree to pay $5 million to Spain toward any claims that American citizens in Florida had against the Spanish.

The treaty also defined the western boundary between the United States and Spanish-held territory. With Spain surrendering all claims in the Northwest, Adams secured a U.S. border that stretched from the Atlantic to the Pacific. For his part, Onís came away from the negotiating table with all of Texas west of the Sabine River still firmly in Spanish hands. Spain also retained the areas known as California and New Mexico. These lands included all of the present-day states of California, New Mexico, Nevada, Utah, and Arizona, as well as portions of Wyoming and Colorado.

The Transcontinental Treaty was sent to the Senate for its approval. The agreement was so popular that every senator voted in favor of ratification. Even the senators who had written the scathing report on Jackson's invasion threw their wholehearted support to the treaty. The public was equally enthusiastic. Most Americans focused on the happy news that the United States now controlled Florida. Only later would the treaty become controversial, when people realized that Adams had bargained away Texas, a land that many Southerners coveted, in exchange for the transcontinental border.

TROUBLE WITH SPAIN

Adams's satisfaction in a job well done quickly faded. About two weeks after the treaty signing, President Monroe found out that the king of Spain had made large grants of Florida land to several of his friends. By the terms of the Transcontinental Treaty, the United States would have to honor these grants, thus limiting the amount of land in Florida that could be opened up for American settlement. George Erving had told Adams that the Spanish crown might try to pull off such a maneuver, but Adams, preoccupied with the negotiations, had done nothing to prevent it.

Adams soon heard even worse news. The treaty had been sent to Spain for ratification. What should have been a formality quickly turned into a crisis, however. Although the king supported the treaty, others in his government felt that it gave too much to the United States. The king's response was to do nothing. If Spain left the treaty unsigned, perhaps Spain could also push the United States back to the bargaining table to work out a more advantageous agreement.

Onís was furious. He had spent literally years negotiating with Monroe and Adams. He finally had a treaty that not only resolved the Florida question without embarrassing Spain, but also confirmed Spain's control over Texas. Justifiably proud of his work, Onís was angry that his own government was holding out for better treaty terms—terms that Onís knew Spain would never see.

CONSIDERING ANOTHER INVASION

By fall, Monroe and his cabinet were rethinking their Florida policy. Tired of waiting for Spain to ratify the treaty, both Adams and Calhoun recommended that they force the issue with another military invasion of Florida. Calhoun went as far as to order Jackson to post the U.S. Army's Southern Division along the Florida border. Jackson sent spies into Florida to assess the military strength of the Spanish forces at St. Augustine.

President Monroe feared, however, that Great Britain and other European nations would not look kindly on another American invasion of Spanish lands. He also worried that European allies would perhaps side with Spain in a war over Florida. In the end, the president chose a different tack. He asked Americans to remain patient regarding the Florida issue. In an address to Congress on December 7, 1819, he recommended that the United States deal with Spain with "candor, magnanimity, and honor."[1] He also indirectly accused the Spanish government of dishonorable behavior in holding up the treaty.

In the fall of 1820, a military revolt shook the Spanish government. In the midst of this political upheaval, Spain reconsidered its position on the Transcontinental Treaty. On October 5, 1820, the Spanish government finally ratified the agreement. It even agreed to declare the last-minute Spanish land grants to be null and void.

The treaty was then resubmitted to the U.S. Senate. There, it was ratified again, by an overwhelming margin. On February 22, 1821, exactly two years after Adams's and Onís's signing ceremony, the Transcontinental Treaty was fully ratified. About five months later, on July 17, the official transfer of flags took place in Pensacola. All of Florida was now officially American soil.

JACKSON RETURNS TO FLORIDA

Earlier in 1820, faced with a downturn in the economy, the U.S. government had been forced to make some budget cuts. Secretary of the Treasury William Crawford had pushed hard for Congress to decrease military spending. Although it was a practical solution to a budgetary problem, Crawford's campaign also was politically motivated. As a vehement opponent of Jackson, Crawford wanted to put a check on his power. So did a number of other congressmen.

At the time, the U.S. Army was divided into two divisions: the Southern Division, under Jackson, and the Northern Division, under Major General Jacob Brown. Brown looked at the congressional budget battles and remarked, "[T]here is, I fear, a fixed determination at all hazards to legislate Genl Jackson out of the service."[2] Brown was right. In January 1821, Congress cut military spending and grouped the two divisions into one to save money. Brown took over the single division, and Jackson was out of a job.

President Monroe found a new post for Jackson. In July 1821, he sent Jackson to Florida to serve as its first military governor. Jackson's return to Florida was brief, however. From the moment he arrived, he butted heads with the exiting Spanish governor, José Callava. At one point, Jackson placed Callava in jail. After a few months of fuming and fighting, Jackson resigned the governorship and returned to Tennessee.

A STATE AT LAST

On March 4, 1822, East Florida and a small portion of West Florida were organized as a U.S. territory, a political designation that was a prelude to statehood. The territorial government consisted of a governor, a legislature, and a judiciary. Pensacola was chosen as the capital. The large distance between St. Augustine and Pensacola soon proved to be a problem. Traveling to the territory's second legislative session, the members of a delegation from St. Augustine nearly died after being

After combining a small part of West Florida with East Florida, the U.S. government created one territory, calling it simply Florida. The population began to grow as people from southern states migrated down to establish new plantations. Soon, the officials of the territory began petitioning for statehood. On March 3, 1845, Florida became the twenty-seventh state of the United States.

shipwrecked while on their way to the capital. The legislature then established a new capital at Tallahassee, a town that was roughly an equal distance from Pensacola and St. Augustine.

From the beginning, territorial officials wanted Florida to become a state. By 1838, its population had grown to such a size that it could make a formal petition for statehood. At a territorial convention, representatives drafted a state constitution, which Floridians narrowly voted to accept. The representatives then submitted the constitution to the U.S. Congress.

Gaining statehood was not simple, however. The anti-slavery faction in Congress did not want to admit Florida as a slave state. Only when its admission was balanced by the impending admission of a free state (Iowa) did Congress accept Florida's petition. On March 3, 1845, the process finally was complete. On that day, Florida was admitted to the Union as the twenty-seventh state.

Florida and American History

On February 22, 1819, John Quincy Adams wrote in his diary that this was possibly "the most important day of my life."[1] It was the day on which he and Luis de Onís signed the Transcontinental Treaty that granted the United States control over Florida. Reflecting on the long and peculiar course of events that had led to that moment, he added, "What the consequences may be of the compact this day signed with Spain is known only to he all-wise and all-beneficent disposer of events, who has brought it about in a manner utterly unexpected and by means the most extraordinary and unforeseen."[2] Adams showed foresight in suggesting that only God could know all the ramifications that the acquisition of Florida would have. In fact, the event would have a long and lasting effect on both the history of Florida and the history of the United States.

Encouraged by the Transcontinental Treaty, the U.S. government decided to continue western expansion and initiated a war with Mexico. The two-year conflict ended in victory for the United States, which gained more than 500,000 square miles of new territory that stretched from Texas to California. *Above*, U.S. troops occupy Mexico City.

REDRAWING BOUNDARIES

The Transcontinental Treaty itself had important repercussions. It did more than bring Florida under American control. It also extended the western border of the United States to the Pacific Ocean. From a practical standpoint, the new western boundary allowed Americans to become more involved in sea trade with China and other Asians nations. It also eliminated Spain as a competitor for coveted land in the Pacific Northwest and made Americans more eager than ever to establish an exclusive claim to the area known as the Oregon Country. For the next several decades, that area was occupied jointly by the United States and Great Britain. The dispute about the land was finally settled in 1846 with the Oregon Treaty, which set the northwestern border between the United States and British-held Canada at the 49th parallel.

By extending the western border of the United States to the Pacific, the Transcontinental Treaty encouraged public enthusiasm for policies aimed at American expansion. Expansionists eventually claimed that it was inevitable that the United States would stretch across the North American continent, a concept often called Manifest Destiny. The acquisition of Florida also taught a lesson to later expansionists. They recognized that Spanish control over their lands in North America was tenuous at best. Even more important, the expansionists learned that even a modest show of American military strength was enough to pluck valuable lands from Spain's grasp.

The expansionist spirit helped fuel support for another war. This war was with Mexico, a country that gained its independence from Spain in 1821. With its victory in the Mexican-American War (1846–1848), the United States established control of all of the present-day states of California, Nevada, and Utah and portions of Wyoming, Colorado, New Mexico, and Arizona.

Another consequence of the Transcontinental Treaty was the conflict over Texas. The treaty allowed Spain, and later Mexico, to retain control of Texas. That did not stop Americans from coveting this area, however. In many ways, the events surrounding the acquisition of Florida became a template for what would happen in Texas. As in Florida, the Spanish government offered land grants to Americans to settle in Texas. As in West Florida, these American settlers eventually rebelled against foreign rule. The Texas rebels established the Republic of Texas in 1836. It lasted far longer than the short-lived Republic of West Florida: Nine years would pass before it entered the Union as the state of Texas.

CHANGES IN WASHINGTON

The events surrounding the acquisition of Florida had an effect on the way politics were conducted in Washington. Jackson had ignored the constitutional requirement that only Congress has the authority to declare war. In turn, Congress chose to ignore Jackson's violation of the Constitution. Because of Congress's unwillingness to confront the issue, future presidents were more willing to run roughshod over Congress's war-making powers. Since the early nineteenth century, American presidents have ordered military actions against foreign powers hundreds of times without bothering to get the approval of Congress.

America's justifications for such military adventures owe a great deal to Adams's Erving letter. By painting American actions as inherently good, Adams helped to shape the rhetoric that many politicians have borrowed since to persuade the American people to support military campaigns, especially those aimed at expanding the United States geographically.

Florida's acquisition also was a pivotal moment in the political lives of the men who made it possible. It was one of the major accomplishments of James Monroe and contributed to his reputation as a president particularly skilled in foreign affairs. For John Quincy Adams, the acquisition of Florida was an enormous triumph, perhaps the greatest in his career as secretary of state. In fact, his role in the negotiation of the Transcontinental Treaty and in the formation of the Monroe Doctrine have secured him a reputation as one of the finest diplomats in all of American history.

Adams's role in the Florida controversy also helped to rehabilitate the reputation of Andrew Jackson. Despite his many supporters, Jackson had alienated quite a few powerful men in Washington—men who would have loved to see Jackson vanish from the political scene. A court-martial of Jackson for his unauthorized excursion into Florida would have tarnished his image as a war hero and perhaps ended any hopes he had to pursue a national political career.

To a large extent, Adams saved Jackson from that disgrace. With the Erving letter, he gave Jackson's supporters the argument they needed, not only to excuse his actions in Florida, but also to bolster up his reputation as a great American patriot. Because Florida's fate and Jackson's fortunes were so deeply intertwined, Adams was willing to risk his own reputation to save Jackson's. As a result, Jackson emerged from the Florida controversy a more popular public figure than ever.

ADAMS VERSUS JACKSON

Florida's acquisition enhanced both Adams's and Jackson's reputations. In 1824, as Monroe's second term drew to an end, the two men were the leading contenders for the presidency. Adams and Jackson were joined in the race by Speaker of the House Henry Clay and Secretary of the Treasury William Crawford.

When the votes were in, Secretary of War John C. Calhoun emerged as vice president. With four men running for president, however, no single candidate had gained a majority of the electoral votes. As a result, the members of the House of Representatives had to decide the election. They did this by considering only the three top candidates: Jackson, with 99 electoral votes; Adams, with 84; and Crawford, with 41.

With only 37 electoral votes, Henry Clay was out of the race, but he was still very much a force in the election. Since taking to the floor of the House to rebuke Jackson for his Florida campaign, Clay had lost none of his ill-will toward the general. Now he was determined that Jackson should not win the presidency. Behind the scenes, Clay threw his support toward Adams. This maneuver allowed Adams to snatch the presidency away from Jackson. Adams then chose Clay as his replacement for secretary of state.

ADAMS IN THE WHITE HOUSE

Adams's term as president was fairly undistinguished. It also was tainted by the lingering anger of Jackson's supporters, who felt that Adams, with Clay's help, had effectively stolen the election. During Adams's four years in office, Jackson's backers staged an unrelenting campaign against the president in the hope that, in

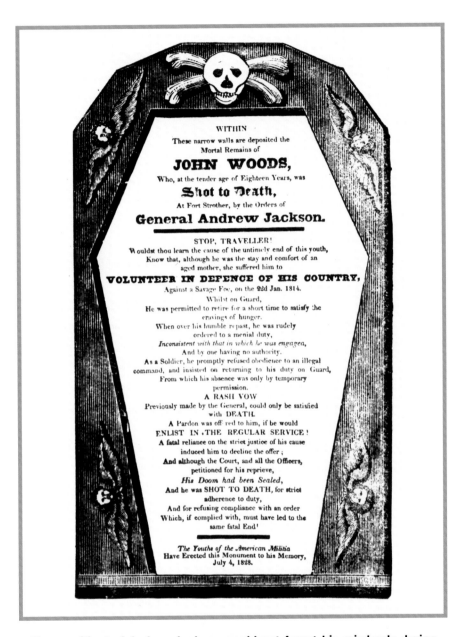

WITHIN
These narrow walls are deposited the
Mortal Remains of

JOHN WOODS,

Who, at the tender age of Eighteen Years, was

Shot to Death,

At Fort Strother, by the Orders of

General Andrew Jackson.

STOP, TRAVELLER!
Wouldst thou learn the cause of the untimely end of this youth,
Know that, although he was the stay and comfort of an
aged mother, she suffered him to

VOLUNTEER IN DEFENCE OF HIS COUNTRY,

Against a Savage Foe, on the 22d Jan. 1814.
Whilst on Guard,
He was permitted to retire for a short time to satisfy the
cravings of hunger.
When over his humble repast, he was rudely
ordered to a menial duty,
Inconsistent with that in which he was engaged,
And by one having no authority.
As a Soldier, he promptly refused obedience to an illegal
command, and insisted on returning to his duty on Guard,
From which his absence was only by temporary
permission.
A RASH VOW
Previously made by the General, could only be satisfied
with DEATH.
A Pardon was offered to him, if he would
ENLIST IN THE REGULAR SERVICE!
A fatal reliance on the strict justice of his cause
induced him to decline the offer ;
And although the Court, and all the Officers,
petitioned for his reprieve,
His Doom had been Sealed,
And he was SHOT TO DEATH, for strict
adherence to duty,
And for refusing compliance with an order
Which, if complied with, must have led to the
same fatal End!

The Youths of the American Militia
Have Erected this Monument to his Memory,
July 4, 1828.

Those critical of Andrew Jackson could not forget his misdeeds during the takeover of Spanish Florida and reminded the general of his mistakes when he ran for president. *Above*, a woodcut of a coffin made during the 1828 presidential election to remind the public of Jackson's execution of militia deserters.

the next election, they would be able to correct the wrongs of the past and place their own man in the White House.

As Andrew Jackson geared up for the 1828 presidential campaign, questions still lingered about his Florida invasion. In an attempt to justify himself, Jackson came up with an entirely new explanation for why he had done what he did. He claimed that after he wrote Monroe to ask permission to seize Florida from Spain, the president responded with a note. According to Jackson, that note, delivered by Tennessee congressman John Rhea, gave him explicit authorization to proceed. He also said that he could not produce the Rhea letter because he had burned it.

Jackson most likely made up the story of the Rhea letter. After all, if the story was true, why did he not bring it up during the congressional investigations into his conduct? That Jackson felt obligated, nearly 10 years later, to come up with further justification for his actions in Florida testifies to how the matter continued to trouble people, even those lawmakers who had cleared him of all wrongdoing. In Washington, throughout the corridors of power, there remained a sense that justice had not been done.

FLORIDA AND JACKSON'S PRESIDENCY

Despite these misgivings, Jackson won the presidency decisively in 1828. This relegated Adams to the list of one-term presidents. After a brief retirement from politics, Adams ran successfully for the House of Representatives in 1831. He held his seat until his death in 1848. Adams's second career in Congress was much more notable than his presidency. He proved a strong voice for the anti-slavery movement. He also was an important opponent of the annexation of Texas and of the Mexican-American War. Ironically, the man who had worked so hard to justify the morally dubious land grab in Florida later became one of the country's foremost critics of American expansionism.

In several ways, Jackson's invasion of Florida had an effect on his presidency. After he took office, Jackson learned that his vice president, John C. Calhoun, had called for Jackson to be censured during closed-door cabinet meetings with President Monroe in 1818. Jackson became furious and started to feud with Calhoun. Their intense dislike for each other contributed to a national crisis in 1832. Calhoun supported the refusal of his home state, South Carolina, to pay a federal tariff. Jackson responded by asking Congress for permission to send troops into the state to enforce the tariff law. In a compromise measure, Congress lowered the tariff, thereby averting an armed conflict within U.S. borders.

The animosity between Henry Clay and Andrew Jackson, fueled in part by the Florida controversy, only grew stronger. In 1832, Jackson defeated Clay for the presidency. During Jackson's second term, Clay attacked him for overreaching in his use of presidential powers. This time, Clay's campaign against Jackson earned the president an official censure from Congress.

(continues on page 104)

"ROOTLESS, RESTLESS, SELF-MADE"

A professor, journalist, and eighth-generation Floridian, Diane Roberts is the author of *Dream State* (2004), a humorous history of Florida that draws on her family lore. In the book, Roberts skewers the annual Springtime Parade in Tallahassee, during which, every year, "some property developer" dresses up as Andrew Jackson and rides "a bay gelding down Monroe Street in his gold-epauletted coat and cockaded *chapeau bas,* his Ray-Bans and his Rolex."* Even as she makes fun of this absurd tribute to Florida's past, Roberts concedes that perhaps Jackson "ought to lead our parades": "You could argue that his is the presiding genius of the state: rootless, restless, self-made, a social Darwinist before Darwin."**

(continues)

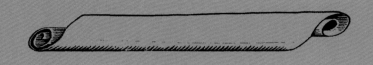

(continued)

In this excerpt from *Dream State,* Roberts provides a satiri-cal account of what Jackson's adventures in Florida meant for her state.

[By 1818, in Florida] it was time for regime change. Secretary of War John C. Calhoun sent Jackson to deliver some shock and awe in the First Seminole War.

Which Jackson did, with a force of 5,000 U.S. soldiers versus 1,300 Seminoles. He violated the international border between U.S. territory and Spanish, ignoring Spanish protests. . . .

Jackson had in mind to besiege the Spanish capital at [St. Augustine]. He'd spread democracy to the southern end of the continent, whether they wanted it or not. He wrote to Calhoun that if the cabinet gave him the high sign, he could conquer all of Florida. . . .

This early-nineteenth-century mission creep was starting to get embarrassing, even to a government full of Monroe Doctrinar-ians. . . . Luis de Onís, Ferdinand VII's minister, and American secretary of state John Quincy Adams quietly started negotiating. President Monroe himself spun Jackson's raids to Congress as protecting the nation. Jackson huffed that he was just trying to 'chastise a savage foe, combined with a lawless band of negro brigands' who prosecuted a 'cruel and unprovoked war against the citizens of the United States' and posed a threat to the Ameri-can Way of Life. His poll numbers shot up. . . .

[Years later, Jackson] was at the center of what is now the quintessential Florida disaster—not a hurricane, but a disputed

presidential election. Jackson won the popular vote, but the electoral college balked at certifying him the victor. The dispute was
kicked into the House of Representatives. . . . The other candidate, John Quincy Adams, a New Englander with a Famous Father,
a Yankee born knowing what fork to use, moved into the White
House.

Jackson sulked in his Tennessee mansion for a while,
reemerging for the election of 1828, ready to kick patrician
butt. . . . This time fighting beat finesse. Jackson rode into
Washington and laid out a philosophy of preemptive violence and a program to get rid of the Indians, especially in
Florida.

The plan was this: Florida was to be a place where
there were two races: whites to own the land, blacks to work
it. . . . The Seminoles, Mikasuikis, Red Sticks, whatever,
had to go. There's never been enough Florida. Everybody
wants a piece—a big piece—for something: cotton, tobacco,
cattle, oranges, sugar cane, phosphate, turpentine, pulp,
resorts, theme parks, suburbs, golf courses, and 'wilderness'
where the last panthers, the last bears, the last eagles, the
totem animals of the Seminoles might find a home. But you
can't go wasting Florida on people who refuse to make a profit
from it.***

---

*Diane Roberts, Dream State: Eight Generations of Swamp Lawyers,
Conquistadors, Confederate Daughters, Banana Republicans, and Other
Florida Wildlife. New York: Free Press, 2004, p. 55.
**Ibid, p. 59.
***Ibid, pp. 58–60.

(continued from page 101)

THE FATE OF THE SEMINOLE

Jackson's history as an "Indian fighter" also came into play during his presidency. With his strong support, the U.S. Congress passed the Indian Removal Act of 1830. This law allowed the federal government to negotiate with the large tribes of the Southeast for their removal (relocation) to lands in the West. Southeasterners hailed Jackson's efforts, which spelled doom for American Indian peoples such as the Creek, the Cherokee, and the Choctaw. Many thousands died on the forced western march. The survivors had to struggle to survive in their strange, new homelands.

Under the jurisdiction of the U.S. government, Jackson's old nemeses, the Seminole of Florida, also were targeted for removal. Many Seminole resisted relocation; they chose, instead, to fight to stay in their traditional territory. The conflict, called the Second Seminole War (1835–1842), was the longest and most expensive war ever fought between an American Indian group and the U.S. Army. Retreating to safety within Florida's swamps, the Seminole staged a guerrilla war, a type of combat in which the American soldiers were not trained to fight effectively. By the end of this costly conflict, most Seminole fighters had surrendered and left for western lands. Some remained in the swamplands, however.

The U.S. Army and the Florida Seminole went to battle one more time, in the Third Seminole War (1855–1858). After this war, the United States gave up on trying to remove the few Seminole still left in Florida. These Seminole essentially won their decades-long struggle. Out of the many American Indians wars fought during the nineteenth century, the Seminole conflict was one of the few lost by the United States.

The Seminole people who remained in Florida not only survived, but thrived. Beginning in the 1920s, they became involved in the Florida tourist industry. The Seminole now operate a variety of profitable businesses, including a casino and golf club. A reflection of the Seminole's integration into Florida

Seminole leader Osceola showed his contempt for the U.S. government by stabbing his knife through a treaty that forced his tribe to surrender most of the lands in present-day Florida. He later fought U.S. forces in the Second Seminole War. In 1837, during peace talks, American troops betrayed Osceola and took him captive as a prisoner of war.

culture, Florida State University, with the tribe's permission, uses the nickname "Seminoles" for their sports teams.

THE SUNSHINE STATE

Of all the consequences of the acquisition of Florida, the most important is also the most obvious: It brought Florida into the Union. Florida became a state in 1845. Ironically, in view of the long effort to incorporate Florida into the United States, it remained under the American flag for only 16 years. In 1861, Florida joined other Southern states in seceding from the Union to form the Confederate States of America. During the American Civil War (1861–1865), Florida was largely uninvolved in the fighting, although a few coastal cities were overtaken by Union troops.

After the defeat of the Confederacy, Florida once again became part of the United States. Socially and economically, however, it remained a backwater until the 1880s. At that time, new railroads connected Florida with the rest of the country, which encouraged more people to settle there.

Florida had to wait for the twentieth century to see real growth. Railroads and, later, automobiles brought more and more Americans to the state. Many people were attracted by the rich farmland. Others were draw by the sunny weather. The number of Floridians rapidly swelled, especially after the state became a popular place for older Americans to retire. Since the 1960s, Florida also has attracted a huge number of immigrants, especially from Cuba and other Caribbean islands. By 2000, Florida was home to nearly 16 million people. It was then the fourth-highest-ranking state in terms of population.

This rapid growth was due, in large part, to the development of the tourism industry. Visitors have long been lured to Florida by its beautiful beaches. More recently, the state has boasted a wealth of man-made attractions as well. These include Disney World and many other theme parks. Each year, these attractions bring tourists from across the country and around the world to the Sunshine State, as does the exciting multicultural atmosphere of Florida's largest city, Miami.

In Miami, Florida might seem like a world in which everything is new. Elsewhere, however, Florida's history—the longest of any U.S. state—is still evident. Nowhere is this truer than in St. Augustine. Founded almost 450 years ago, this oldest city in America houses the remains of structures that speak of Florida's colorful past—a past shared by the American Indians, Spanish, French, British, and Americans who, at one time or another, called Florida their home.

CHRONOLOGY

1513   **April 2** Spanish conquistador Juan Ponce de León
       arrives on the coast of what is now Florida.

1565   **September 8** Pedro Menéndez de Avilés founds the
       Spanish town of St. Augustine.

1763   **February 10** Spain surrenders Florida to the British
       following the French and Indian War; the British
       divide the area into East and West Florida.

TIMELINE

April 2, 1513
Spanish conquistador
Juan Ponce de León
arrives on the coast of
what is now Florida

September 16, 1810
American settlers in Baton
Rouge form the Republic
of West Florida; 11 weeks
later, the United States
occupies the area

1513

1812

February 10, 1763
Spain surrenders
Florida to the British
following the French
and Indian War; the
British divide the area
into East and West
Florida

September 3, 1783
Spain regains control
over both East and
West Florida after the
American Revolution

March 1812
Former Georgia
governor George
Mathews invades
East Florida, ini-
tiating the Patriot
War

1783 **September 3** Spain regains control over both East and West Florida after the American Revolution.

1795 **October 27** Pinckney's Treaty formalizes the border between Spanish Florida and the United States.

1804 **Summer** The Kemper brothers lead an unsuccessful popular rebellion against Spanish rule in West Florida.

1810 **September 16** American settlers in Baton Rouge form the Republic of West Florida; 11 weeks later, the United States occupies the area.

1812 **March** Former Georgia governor George Mathews invades East Florida, initiating the Patriot War.

January 1819
Congress begins debating the constitutionality of Jackson's invasion of Florida

February 22, 1821
The Transcontinental Treaty is ratified by the United States and Spain

1818 ———— 1845

March 12, 1818
Jackson invades Florida during the First Seminole War

February 8, 1819
Members of the House of Representatives vindicate Jackson of all wrongdoing relating to the Florida controversy

March 3, 1845
Florida becomes the twenty-seventh state to enter the Union

1812–1814 The United States battles Great Britain in the War of 1812.

1812–1813 U.S. general Andrew Jackson wages war against the Upper Creeks.

1816 **July 27** American and Creek forces invade East Florida and destroy Negro Fort, a refuge for runaway slaves.

1817 **June 29** Scottish adventurer Gregor MacGregor takes over Amelia Island, off the coast of East Florida.

December 28 President James Monroe writes to General Andrew Jackson, giving him the authority to head into Florida to battle Seminole Indians.

1818 **March 12** Jackson invades Florida during the First Seminole War.

May 23 Without the authority of Congress, Jackson takes over the Spanish fort at Pensacola.

December 28 The Erving Letter, written by Secretary of State John Quincy Adams to justify Jackson's invasion of Spanish Florida, is published in the United States.

1819 **January** Congress begins debating the constitutionality of Jackson's invasion of Florida.

February 8 Members of the House of Representatives vindicate Jackson of all wrongdoing relating to the Florida controversy.

February 22 John Quincy Adams and Spanish diplomat Luis de Onís sign the Transcontinental Treaty.

1821 **February 22** The Transcontinental Treaty is ratified by the United States and Spain.

July 17 The United States formally takes control of East and West Florida.

1845 **March 3** Florida becomes the twenty-seventh state to enter the Union.

Notes

CHAPTER 1
1. Robert V. Remini, *Andrew Jackson and His Indian Wars.* New York: Viking, 2001, 148.
2. Ibid.
3. Ibid, 149.
4. Ibid, 150.
5. Ibid, 155.
6. Ibid, 154.
7. David S. Heidler and Jeanne T. Heidler, *Old Hickory's War: Andrew Jackson and the Quest for Empire.* Baton Rouge: Louisiana State University Press, 2003, 154.

CHAPTER 2
1. Michael Gannon, *Florida: A Short History.* Gainesville: University Press of Florida, 2003, 17.
2. Ibid, 23.
3. Ibid.

CHAPTER 3
1. Gannon, 26.

CHAPTER 4
1. Andrew H. Scott, "Between 1810 and 1821, The United State Acquired Florida by a Protracted Campaign to Subvert Spanish Rule," *Military History.* vol. 15, no. 4 (October 1998), 21.
2. Ibid.

3. Michael Gannon, ed., *The New History of Florida.* Gainesville: University Press of Florida, 1996, 163.

CHAPTER 5
1. Heidler, 91.
2. William Earl Weeks, *John Quincy Adams and American Global Empire.* Lexington: The University Press of Kentucky, 1992, 62.
3. Ibid, 109.
4. Ibid.

CHAPTER 6
1. Weeks, 113.

CHAPTER 7
1. Weeks, 144.
2. Ibid, 142.
3. Ibid, 145.
4. Ibid, 158.
5. Ibid, 159.
6. Heidler, 216.
7. Weeks, 168.

CHAPTER 8
1. Weeks, 173.
2. Heidler, 229.

CHAPTER 9
1. Weeks, 166.
2. Ibid.

BIBLIOGRAPHY

Cusick, James G. *The Other War of 1812: The Patriot War and the American Invasion of Spanish East Florida.* Athens: The University of Georgia Press, 2003.

Gannon, Michael. *Florida: A Short History.* Gainesville: University Press of Florida, 2003.

———. ed. *The New History of Florida.* Gainesville: University Press of Florida, 1996.

Heidler, David S., and Jeanne T. Heidler. *Old Hickory's War: Andrew Jackson and the Quest for Empire.* Baton Rouge: Louisiana State University Press, 2003.

McMichael, Andrew. "The Kemper 'Rebellion': Filibustering and Resident Anglo American Loyalty in Spanish West Florida." *Louisiana History* vol. 43, no. 2 (2002): 133–165.

Remni, Robert V. *Andrew Jackson and His Indian Wars.* New York: Viking, 2001.

Scott, Andrew H. "Between 1810 and 1821, The United States Acquired Florida by a Protracted Campaign to Subvert Spanish Rule." *Military History* vol. 15, no. 4 (October 1998): 20–21.

Weeks, William Earl. *John Quincy Adams and American Global Empire.* Lexington: The University Press of Kentucky, 1992.

Further Reading

Behrman, Carol H. *Andrew Jackson.* Minneapolis: Lerner Publications, 2003.

Greene, Meg. *The Transcontinental Treaty, 1819.* New York: Rosen Publishing Group, 2005.

Levy, Debbie. *James Monroe.* Minneapolis: Lerner Publications, 2005.

————. *John Quincy Adams.* Minneapolis: Lerner Publications, 2005.

McCarthy, Kevin. *Native Americans in Florida.* Sarasota, Fla.: Pineapple Press, 1999.

Mountjoy, Shane. *St. Augustine.* New York: Chelsea House, 2007.

Sonneborn, Liz. *The War of 1812.* New York: Rosen Publishing Group, 2004.

West, Patsy. *The Enduring Seminoles: From Alligator Wrestling to Casino Gambling.* rev. ed. Gainesville: University Press of Florida, 2008.

WEB SITES

Florida Historical Map Collection

www.uflib.ufl.edu/spec/pkyonge/fhmaps.html

Maintained by the University of Florida, this site includes images of historical maps of Florida that show the region's changing borders from the sixteenth through the nineteenth century.

The Florida Memory Project

www.floridamemory.com

The State Library and Archives of Florida presents a selection of
photographs and documents relating to Florida history, as well
as a useful timeline.

Floridiana on the Web

www.lib.usf.edu/ldsu/digitalcollections/F03/html/index.html

The University of South Florida Libraries have assembled this
searchable online resource that features documents, pictures,
and audio and video recordings dealing with Florida history and
culture.

The Hermitage

www.thehermitage.com

The Hermitage was the Tennessee home of Andrew Jackson.
The mansion and its grounds are now a museum. The Web site
includes a detailed biography of Jackson and pictures of items
on display at the Hermitage.

Louisiana: European Explorations and the Louisiana Purchase

www.memory.loc.gov/ammem/collections/maps/lapurchase/
index.html

This essay, illustrated with historic maps from the collection of
the Library of Congress, discusses the history of the Louisiana
Territory under Spanish, French, and American rule. The essay
is part of the Library of Congress's online American Memory
collection.

St. Augustine: America's Ancient City

www.flmnh.ufl.edu/staugustine/intro.htm

This site, created by the Florida Museum of Natural History,
offers an illustrated timeline of the history of the city of St.
Augustine under Spanish rule.

Seminole People of Florida: Survival and Success

www.flheritage.com/museum/mfh/exhibits/seminole

A companion to an exhibit at the Museum of Florida History, this
site features a history of the Seminole in Florida and provides

links to images and further information about the Seminole
people.

Spanish Colonization of Florida

www.hmsf.org/exhibits/sf/sf.htm

This online exhibition from the Historical Museum of Southern
Florida offers a brief summary of the Spanish era in Florida,
accompanied by artwork relating to the period.

Photo Credits

PAGE

 2: © National Portrait Gallery/Art Resource

 6: North Wind Picture Archive/Alamy

12: North Wind Picture Archive/Alamy

15: The Granger Collection, New York

19: Infobase Publishing

27: © Erich Lessing/Art Resource

30: Bridgeman Art Library

39: The Granger Collection, New York

42: The Granger Collection, New York

51: Bridgeman Art Library

58: HIP/Art Resource

62: Bettmann/Corbis

65: Bridgeman Art Library

73: North Wind Pictures

77: Bridgeman Art Library

81: Bridgeman Art Library

85: Infobase Publishing

92: The Band/www.shutterstock.com

95: Bridgeman Art Library

99: The Granger Collection, New York

105: Bridgeman Art Library

INDEX

ABOUT THE AUTHOR

LIZ SONNEBORN is a writer living in Brooklyn, New York. A graduate of Swarthmore College, she has written more than 60 books for children and adults, including *The American West, The Gold Rush, A to Z of American Indian Women, The Mexican-American War, The Mormon Trail,* and *Chronology of American Indian History.*